INVADER
MOON

WHO BROUGHT US THE MOON AND WHY?

ROB SHELSKY

A PERMUTED PRESS BOOK

ISBN: 978-1-61868-666-4
ISBN (eBook): 978-1-61868-665-7

INVADER MOON
Who Brought Us the Moon and Why?
© 2016 by Rob Shelsky
All Rights Reserved

Cover art by Quincy Alivio

PERMUTED
PRESS

Permuted Press LLC
275 Madison Avenue, 6th Floor
New York, NY 10016
http://permutedpress.com

**DEDICATED
IN MEMORIAM
TO**

GEORGE A. KEMPLAND

*Wherever You Are Now, George,
May You Always Be Happy, At Peace, And Enjoying
Yourself.
I Hope I May Get To See You Again...Somewhen.*

CONTENTS

PART FOUR—THE ENDING

INTRODUCTION

Could there really have been a time "before there was a Moon"? Was there really the arrival of an "Invader Moon" in our skies? Was this the result of a battle beyond the stars, as well as here on Earth? Did it cause a worldwide major catastrophe of truly epic proportions?

Fire from the sky?

A sudden melting of the Ice Age glaciers?

Global cataclysmic flooding?

The rise of humanity out of the ashes of the old world of the alien invaders?

A subsequent loss of our racial memory of any of this having occurred?

Finally, why does the date of 10,000 BCE, 12,000 years ago, keep popping up in all sorts of ways when it comes to all this?

Do all these questions sound too bizarre and just not part of real history? Well, perhaps it's not a part of history as we know it, but then, we are always finding out more about our history as time goes by. This is the case here. There is another history, one long forgotten, or perhaps even suppressed.

Consider this statement: "History is written by the winners." Most of us have heard this said at one time or another. The implication is, of course, that those who win the wars get to write the history of such things from their perspective. It is not worth arguing this point, because I happen to think it is true enough.

However, have you ever stopped to think that those who have forgotten their heritage also write history? Take a people and transplant them to a new location, or even new circumstances, without any means of recording their past, and those people will have to write a whole new history about themselves. Or if they don't have the means of writing it, then they must pass it on some other way, by handing it down as an oral history over the ages, for example.

Often this history is based on what meager evidence they still have and, when people are in hard times, struggling and scrabbling just to survive, maintaining such evidence is not a top priority. Racial memory of events is often minimal as a result. The very disaster they have had to endure causes this loss of memory of that disaster.

Therein lies a problem. By today's rigorous scientific standards, if the evidence isn't enough, isn't corroborated, then the archaeologists and historians of our era say that such oral histories are only a partial history, loaded with errors, or just plain wrong. For most modern historical researchers, oral histories are just "legends and myths," and not to be taken seriously at all. Yet the people who took the time to hand those down from one generation to the next took them seriously enough to make such an effort.

There is another problem: cultural bias. We in the West are very good at thinking of our oral histories as being at least partially factual, while those "legends" of the East are just pure fiction. In other words, we have a cultural prejudice of what we accept as orally handed down stories being mostly true or not true at all. Many of ours are, therefore, but not others, those not "ours."

For instance, western historians always refer to the "myths and legends" of the Hindus of India. Where these people see their ancient vedic texts as real historical texts, written ones, no less, we in Western Civilization have seen them as just mere legends, myths, and "not real events." For us, they are just so many fantasies and fantastical fictions.

Tens of thousands of lines of historical texts, and we never even bothered to see if they held any validity at all! Yet, whoever wrote all of them, put forth such enormous effort to record all of those texts, certainly they must have felt it was worthwhile to spend thousands of person-hours to do so!

Cultural bias or not, the question remains, is their version of past events just fanciful myths, or are they largely true? Is there far more to the history of the human race than our historians and archaeologists will allow, or even consider? Are ancient aliens involved? Is there evidence the Moon was not always in our sky? Did something momentous take place about 12,000 years ago? The magic date of 10,000 BCE does keep cropping up and that is a fact.

These questions, we will attempt to answer here in this book, *Invader Moon*. Because, you see, I think we have it wrong, very wrong. Our history is incomplete, and in my opinion often comes to erroneous conclusions.

Our version of our past, the one pounded into us repeatedly in school, is that civilization, real civilization, only came into being after the ending of the last major glacial period of the Ice Age. Furthermore, that civilization then started in one location, the Middle East, and then somehow occurred virtually simultaneously around the world at an astonishing rate, one so fast it has been referred to as an "explosion," or being "overnight." This "explosion" is one for which we cannot account, or find a trigger. From this sudden beginning, our civilization has evolved to its current technological level, and according to archaeologists and historians, is the first to have ever done so. Today's worldwide civilization is the first—they say.

Or is it? In the following pages, we are going to see that this is not the case. We will discover that history, as it now stands and based on current archaeological theories is not only coming under increasing attack, but often has to be rewritten to include new information. Everything we thought we knew about our history may be based on one huge fallacy—too much missing information about its beginning. Our version of the human past needs a complete rewriting.

Why? Because we have much more information than we did even twenty years ago.

From the evidence gathered, it is clear we need to revise out thinking about humanity's true history. Again, why? Because it is my, as well as many other researchers' contention that not only is civilization on Earth much older than originally thought, but there were two distinct civilizations, ours, and one before ours.

Moreover, this older civilization was not born of this Earth. Rather this antediluvian culture came from elsewhere, and at some point, our Moon came along with it. Not only were there extraterrestrials who invaded our Earth, but there was our Invader Moon, which conquered our skies, as well.

Again, does this sound fantastical, farfetched? Well, read on, and I think you will find the idea really isn't so crazy at all. In fact, it would explain many things!

In addition, there seems to be a lot of evidence for this idea, this new version of human history. This book will show strong evidence for the statements above, will draw from a variety of sources for evidence. *Invader Moon* won't rely on just one type of proof, but that of three main types:

1. There will be evidence from physical sources, archaeological ones, as well as those from the other hard sciences. This evidence will be from sources around the world.

2. There will be evidence included from written historical records, actual historical documents. This, too, will come from sources around the globe.

3. Where appropriate, this book will include oral traditions and stories, but with the caveat that they must have extensive corroboration of similar tales from around the world.

Notice, there is great emphasis for all this evidence, despite its nature, as having to come from around the globe, be worldwide in nature. This is because whatever happened on Earth appears to have been a planet-wide event, and so logically, evidence for it should come from different places.

Finally, for the first time, this book attempts to put all we know about all these subjects into one context, to form on ultimate picture of events on a timeline of history, as it really happened. This is the trust of this book. This is a bit like using all the pieces of a jigsaw puzzle we can find to create a final and true depiction of our history. As always, it will be left to the reader to judge if this ultimate picture is a believable and reliable scenario, based on the available evidence.

Therefore, in the final analysis, it will be up to the readers to make their own decisions if enough evidence has been supplied to do the job. Now, let us start assembling the great historical puzzle of our *Invader Moon* by establishing the framework for our picture and let us find out if there really were extraterrestrials, if the Moon is an invader in our skies, and just what really did happen in 10,000 BCE, 12,000 years ago!

CHAPTER 1

WHAT DO WE KNOW?

We've all heard, seen, and read a lot about ancient aliens. How could we not these days? Such shows seem to be everywhere on television. With this enormous influx of information, we often find it hard to make any sense of it all, to be able to sift through the facts versus the merely suggestive.

Yet, some information, especially some gathered these last few years, is highly important. I'm speaking of such things as actual satellite photo images of Earth, as well as other sources of data. This is hard evidence, and it is mounting in volume with each passing year.

However, what seems to be lacking is putting all of this various information into some kind of real context, some order that helps us to understand things better, and so bring us up to date on it all. We have the pieces of a puzzle, but no clear overall picture.

As an example, the information with regard to the idea ancient aliens actually existed is overwhelming and often complex. Moreover, it is all over the place. We're told about this find, or that artifact, or some other pictogram on a rock somewhere. The television shows often jump all around in time with regard to these things, sometimes, spanning centuries, and sometimes, crossing millennia. Often, what they produce as evidence isn't really evidence at all, but just a series of surmises based on very flimsy bits of information. Other times, the evidence seems quite solid and reliable.

Then there is the matter of all the other aspects to this. What would these aliens be doing on earth, if they did come? Why did they come here? What reasons do they have for staying, if they are still staying here? If they have left—why? Moreover, just what does the moon have to do with all of this, because it seems to have played a big part in whatever all this is about.

So just how do we arrive at any conclusions, let alone ones we can trust? Well, there are a number of ways.

1. We want to use the best available evidence, and as much of the newest reliable data we can find, as well.

2. We have to put the many pieces of this jigsaw puzzle together in such a way that we can get an overall picture, one that makes sense, if possible.

3. Then we can make better guesses about what might still be missing from the puzzle and so be able reliably to fill in some of what may still be missing.

Why even bother? Well, we need to have answers to these questions. All of them! Again, why? Well, not to know our true past means continuing to make some very false and wrong assumptions about it. This is always a dangerous thing to do, because of possible and unforeseen repercussions. Decisions based on false data can be, and sometimes are, disastrous.

Then there is the matter of our future. How do we go forward when we don't even know what our real past might have been? How do we avoid making the same mistakes again, if we don't know the ones we've already made?

Furthermore, our past may hold some terrible and powerful secrets we've forgotten, or been "made" to forget. If this is so, we need to know what they are, if only for survival's sake, to know what we might be up against. Can this be done? Can we arrive at the answers we so desperately need?

Well, the answer is yes, but we have to do it systematically. We need to:

1. Include the most telling factors about all these topics, the most reliable pieces of evidence. We need to know which ones are of the most importance, and which are of the least, and which don't matter at all. We can't do this with every single piece of evidence, of course, because the truth is, there is just too much of it. Even so, we can do it with the overall idea of using each "type" of evidence and then uses major examples of each to present our case here.

2. We need to take all this information and sort it into main categories. For instance, the Moon—we need to have an understanding of where this satellite of ours belongs in all this. If you haven't guessed by now, I think the Moon plays a big part. There are just too many strange things about our Moon, many of which I have covered in a prior book, *For The Moon Is Hollow And Aliens Rule The Sky*. However, in this book, the sequel, I'm going to focus on just how the moon is involved in all of this, specifically, with regard to our history, what effect the Moon had on it and still does, rather than just the Moon itself.

3. Speaking of history, this is our next major item, one we also need to put into perspective. As I mentioned earlier, many of the television shows about ancient aliens seem to jump around through time in the most annoying ways. One minute, we are in 1500 BCE (Before Common Era). A few minutes later, and we might be 8000 years ago or even further into the past. This is confusing and such a method doesn't make it easy to put things into context, to make sense of them and see them in their proper perspective. We need to do that, to get events in their proper order.

4. We must create a timeline of events. This timeline will grow as we add our pieces of the puzzle to it. When finished, if pieces are still missing, we can then make better deductions about them, their exact nature. A timeline also does another very important thing, for it shows us if some events are just a little too "coincidental" to be that, just mere coincidences.

By using these methods, we should be able to arrive at some solid and perhaps very important conclusions. For example, we should be able to establish the extent of the Moon's influence on events on Earth, when and how our celestial neighbor may have interfered in them, and what the ultimate outcome of such interference might have been.

The final step in the process of creating a whole from the parts is then to show evidence from various sources proving the points placed on the timeline. For example, if there was a worldwide civilization, the so-called "Pre-Adamite" civilization, then there must be evidence for such a thing. That evidence must be found in locations around the Earth in order to prove such a civilization was, indeed, worldwide. Finding evidence in just one or two locations would not be sufficient to support such a theory. Evidence must be more widespread.

The same holds true for the idea of a Great Flood. Luckily, with that topic, we have already have had much evidence produced. However, it is a major point of contention among various factions in and out of science, as to just when this might have taken place and to what extent. In addition, the circumstances under which it took place are also a question. Was it just a big flood, or was there more to it? The Bible speaks of rain preceding the deluge. Do we have any real evidence for such a thing having actually happened? Did anything else happen at the same time?

Of course, the most vital thing in all of this is how it affected us, humankind. Were we a "bad" people and so struck down by an angry God, made to start all over again, as the Bible would have us believe? Or were we the people who were even struck down? Might it have been somebody else? If so, where were we and what were we doing during all of this? What caused the Great Flood?

Was it a natural event? If it was unnatural, then why did "they," whoever "they" were, inflict such a thing upon the world?

We have to have evidence for all of this and I think we do. In the following pages, I tend to categorize this evidence, add it to a timeline, and try to put it all in context. This includes everything from the Moon in our sky, to the possibility of the existence of Atlantis and other lost civilizations. I intend to show the whole world was involved in a major catastrophe, one in which the Moon played a great role.

I also intend to show that not only was Atlantis destroyed by the events of this time, but other civilizations, as well. Somebody or some "thing" was picking and choosing civilizations, or so it is my belief. I intend to supply evidence for this belief.

There are many things to consider, and now it's time to get to work. We will start with part one, the beginning of the timeline. We will discuss the civilization that existed and died before our own came into being. Now, we'll see if we have proof of this, as well.

We will start our timeline with what mainstream archaeologists say is the time of the "overnight explosion" of modern civilization. This is our first marker on the timeline.

PART ONE

THE TIMELINE BEGINS

5500 Years Ago

2015 CE

Figure 1: Timeline Begins For Rise of Modern Civilization 5500 years ago.
First Cities Appear, Then Concept Of Empires And Ultimately, Nation States Of Today.

CHAPTER 2

THE GREAT STAGNANT PERIOD

How did civilization begin and when? That's a major question in itself, because it seems there were several beginnings. We want to go back to what is believed to be the start of things eventually, though, and this is the time of the "Pre-Adamites." They are named this simply because they existed before the time of Adam and Eve, the so-called first humans.

Let me introduce a major caveat here. This is not a religious book in nature, or in any sense of that term. I use the phrase, "Pre-Adamites" here, as just a means of easy reference to a specific people and time, but not as having any religious meaning in any way implied by using this term. "Pre-Adamites" is strictly used for convenience only with no religious overtones implied.

"But nobody could exist before Adam," you say? He was, after all the first man. Right?

Well, first, for those who don't believe in the Bible as the literal word of God, this isn't a problem to believe such a thing. It's easy for those of a secular perspective, such as me, to think there were others before the first true humans, as we think of ourselves.

Neanderthals, for example, might well be defined as "Pre-Adamites" under such conditions, although, there is strong DNA evidence they were genetically so close to us, we could interbreed with them and apparently have. Those of European origin have anywhere from one to four percent, on average, Neanderthal DNA in them to prove this.

But just what do we know about "Pre-Adamites?" Did they even actually exist, and if so when? Well, we know they have to have existed before our current civilization began recording its history, since we have no written records of it, and in order to meet the term of "Pre-Adamite."

If so, when was this? When did the Pre-Adamite civilization begin and end? Well, it is my contention and that of other researchers that the Pre-Adamite civilization ended around 12,000 years ago, or about 10,000 BCE. As to when it began, that we researchers are less certain about, but we'll get into that a little later on in this book. In the meantime, let's look at some of the evidence that supports the idea of when their civilization expired and ours began.

What We Know (Or Think We Know):

1. Most archaeologists/scientists agree that our civilization rose after the end of the last major glacial period of the Ice Age. Scientists say massive ice sheets on the North American Continent, as well as Eurasia, principally characterized the last such major glaciation. These peaked at different times. Glaciers often advanced and withdrew. However, overall, this last glaciation period was from 110,000 to 12,000 years ago, and so ended about 12,000 years ago, or 10,000 BCE.

2. Most archaeologists, and by that we mean practically all of them, believe that civilization as we now know it, started sometime around 3500 BCE. this was when the beginning of the rise of modern concepts, such as the idea of the "state" and "cities" began. Prior to this, according to those same archaeologists, humans lived in small settlements and practiced a primitive and agricultural-based culture. These settlements had very small populations, almost all being well under a hundred, and some being just a handful in size. If not

part of such settlements, other humans were nomadic hunter-gatherers.

What suddenly changed this, most archaeologists still argue about, and rather ceaselessly. No one seems sure just why, about 5500 years ago (3500 BCE), there was a sudden change in this way of life. After all those millennia of, frankly, not much of anything happening, then, "as if overnight," as many archaeologists put it, "civilization exploded." This is also the term many of them use for the rapid rise of civilization. The change came about astonishingly quickly. As to why this was so rapid is another of those hotly debated topics among archaeologists and historians.

3. This means the modern idea of cities and urban centers of population started around 5500 years ago, approximately. Again, this is according to mainstream archaeologists.

4. If civilization started around this time, and the last glacial period of the Ice Age ended 12,000 years ago, we have a long gap where nothing much seems to have taken place. Let's call this gap the "Great Stagnant Period" because, according to archaeologists, nothing much at all in a major way seems to have been going on during all those 6500 years. We will add these points on our timeline at the end of this chapter, so we can begin to see exactly how the flow of events went.

As we can see by our growing timeline (see Title Page, Part Two), we've managed a few of the pieces of the puzzle. The timeline now dates back to 10,000 BCE, or 12,000 years ago. As we move toward the present, we see a gap of 6500 years in which there was no civilization, except in the most basic and rudimentary forms of an agrarian (agricultural) society. Then we have our original marker, 3500 BCE, when civilization as we know it starts.

One of the first things we notice now with our timeline is that Great Stagnant Period, how it stands out, running as it does between the end of the last glacial period and the rise of our current civilization. This is a long, long time when human culture seems to be stagnant and showing no real progress at all. This in itself is curious.

Why? Why such a long time? For those 6500 years, were people incapable of innovation, invention, and learning anything new? Somehow, they learned to use tools for millennia, taught themselves how to grow food, and take care of their basic needs, but then they just stopped acquiring knowledge for over six millennia? That's longer than our current civilization has existed! Again, this seems very strange. What could account for this?

Moreover, what happened to change this state of static affairs? What was the "trigger" that started civilization on the move to what we now have today? This is a puzzle we have yet to answer, or have we? We may have the answer staring us in the face and not even know it.

However let's move on for the moment. I think the best way of replying to our questions is to move back further into the past, beyond that stagnant period in our history, and approach that almost magical seeming number of 10,000 BCE, or 12,000 years ago.

PART TWO

ANCIENT WONDERS

Figure 2: Timeline: Great Stagnant Period Of 6500 Years Before Rise of Modern Civilization At 5500 years ago. Time Span To Present Day: 12,000 Years

CHAPTER 3

PROOF OF AN ANCIENT

CIVILIZATION?

Before our civilization, was there another one? Well, we seem to have a great deal of evidence there was and even more than one civilization, perhaps. So let's look at some of the evidence for such a thing:

There seems to be a great deal of evidence for buildings of a specific nature dating far back into history and long before the rise of modern civilization. This evidence is from around the globe. The bizarre part is that, according to most archaeologists, such buildings shouldn't go back so far in time, at least, not far back past the time of 3500 BCE. However, they do, and by millennia! These include:

1. **Over 8000 Stone Monuments On The Island Of Sardinia— The "Nuraghi."** These almost lighthouse-like structures can be as tall as eighteen meters high, with only one entrance and no windows, or sometimes, just one tiny one. Originally, it is thought there were around 10,000 of them!

Archaeologists theorize these might have been very ancient forts. Yet, there are far too many of them for such a purpose and some seem far too small, as well. Forts, by their nature, are expensive affairs for a civilization that is few in numbers, means, and resources. Not only is there the costs of time and effort in building and maintaining such forts, but then they have to be manned on a regular basis.

For a world with a very small population at the time, 10,000 such forts, with just one person to occupy each of them would be a huge effort. This just makes no logical sense at all. However, some of the structures might well have been fort-like in nature. These particular ones have evidence of corridors and outer walls. As one can see, the Nuraghi structures are by no means all the same in design, but they are all made of stone and most are not fort-like in nature, but rather only a few.

Moreover, if those are forts, many of them were terribly designed ones. With just the one small doorway, and more often than not, no windows, how did one defend them? The enemy could build a roaring fire around the perimeter of them and roast people trapped inside. They could do this with very little effort. The small window existing in some of the Nuraghi was too low and too small to effectively shoot an arrow through. Unless one was aiming at the enemy's feet, they would have been useless for such a purpose. Therefore, it appears highly unlikely that the vast majority of these stone monuments were ever forts.

Rather, it seems far more likely these towers, or monuments, were for some astronomical or perhaps calendar-related purpose. In addition, if so, this gives us the age of such towers. Archaeologists currently think the towers must be anywhere 2000 to 3500 years old, which places their construction at around 1500 BCE, at the most. In fact, the towers would seem far older than that. First, it is impossible to know the age of stone buildings. One can know the age of the stone used in them, but one can't know the age of the building itself, not without other information or sources to tell us.

This means there is no current means of dating the Nuraghi by themselves alone. However, one can often use clues to get an approximation. For example, the windows of the towers that do have them seem to have been aligned with the spring equinox star. However, it is not the star of today, but rather the star, Taurus, which acted as the spring equinox star around some 6000 years ago. This was before the beginning of even the Early Bronze Age, and long before the beginning time of the rise of civilization, according to archaeologists. Therefore, we have literally thousands of "forts" or towers constructed long before they should have been. For this reason, the spring equinox star, some researchers think the buildings are much older, and date back to perhaps 10,000 or even 12,000 years.

2. **Russian "Stonehenge."** Stonehenge in England is considered "*the* Stonehenge," of course, but there are others. In fact, there is around 5000 or more such stone circles around the world. Some form groups of such circles, such as in Senegal, with the Senegambia Circles. These, although counted as just one grouping, as with the rows of stones at Carnac, there are many monuments that make up all these circles, some 1000 or so in all and these cover a vast area. One estimate put the region of the stones as being some 1393.5 square meters in size.

Even Russia is not without its megalithic monuments. There are the Seven Sleeping giants. In addition, well within the borders of what was once the greater Russian empire known as the Soviet Union, there are more. One of the most important of these is Arkaim. Here again, we have one of those extra-mysterious places. Like so many other such sites, considerable debate about the place rages on.

Situated in southern mountains of the Urals, Arkaim isn't a typical "henge," but rather refers to structures forming two walls encircling a settlement. This town or village was approximately 20,439 square meters in area and was an odd-shaped place with twin circles of residences with a street in between them.

Unearthed by archaeologists in 1987, the site is a truly old one, dating back to 1700 BCE. If true, the site dates is close to 4000 years old, with others arguing it is even older. Quite a number of artifacts from the settlement were also unearthed. Despite these other finds, the date when the structure was erected is often a subject of controversy.

There is another reason for controversy concerning Arkaim and it has nothing to do with the dating of the site. This is because, with some mental effort, one can perhaps see the structures within the very center of the walls as being in a sort of swastika design.

There is another problem. Evidence suggests Arkaim was created by an Indo-Iranian group called the Sintashta. Meaning it has close connections to, and ties with the true ancient Aryans, and not the self-proclaimed ones of the Third Reich. However, with this combination, a pseudo-swastika design at the heart of the Arkaim site, and the fact of its founding by the Sintashta makes for rather a volatile combination, politically speaking.

This aside, Arkaim is of interest because it, like Stonehenge, in Wiltshire, England, has strong astronomical connections. So much so, it is more than just a "calendar" in stone to help people know when to plant and harvest crops, but is seen instead, as an actual celestial observatory of sorts. It's a good one, even better than Stonehenge in that regard, having the capability of tracking eighteen different celestial phenomena, whereas Stonehenge only has ten. Not only that, but its precision is quite incredible for such an ancient place.

Now, it is important in all this to remember this is quite a stunning achievement, since it preceded major civilizations in this regard. We're talking about a civilization that should have been nothing more than hunter-gathers at the time, and yet, they had developed and created in their Arkaim, not only a settlement with two circles of stone to protect a larger interior space, but one that was also an observatory—not just a calendar—as well. This is quite something for people who were considered to be little better than cave dwellers!

For this reason, some claim that Arkaim is yet another link to an ancient civilization, one that existed long before our own did, or at least it contained and was built from the lingering knowledge gained from such a civilization. Wherever the knowledge came from is a mystery, since nobody knows how these people came by so much of it, or spent such a prodigious amount of time and effort to build a place not only to live in, but one that acted as an observatory, as well.

3. **Ruins Of Salar De Uyuni.** This is a huge salt flat with areas of saltwater. Salar de Uyuni is the largest salt flat in the world and lies at about 3656 meters above sea level. The lake is in the Alto Plano region of Ecuador/Bolivia. The Salar de Uyuni, between 30,000 and 42,000 years ago, was a vast lake. Now, there are two smaller lakes nearby, Lake Poopó and Uru Uru Lake. Lake Poopó is near to Lake Titicaca, and it receives some of the overflow of this larger lake, and in turn, passes some of this on to the Salar de Uyuni. To grasp the size of this area is not an easy thing to do. The salt flat, in total, covers some 10,582 square kilometers. This means the Salar de Uyuni is huge!

The flat is so large that satellites can observe it. Of course, some images have been taken. These images show ruins in the lake, ancient ones. These structures had to have been built there before the lake became a salt one, because now to attempt such structures would be virtually impossible. The extreme salinity, the deep crusts of salt, would make such construction, even now, doubtful, at best.

Therefore, the ruins had to have been built when the water was still fresh, but more likely, even before the lake formed. This would place the date of the ruins at about 15,000 to 20,000 years ago, approximately, or around 13,000 BCE to as far back as 22,000 BCE. This means they might well have been built during the last glaciation period of our current Ice Age, and many, many millennia before not only modern civilization began (3500 BCE), but even long before the stagnant period of some 6500 years prior to the start of our civilization.

4. **Yoniguni Pyramid.** Most of us have heard about the Yoniguni Pyramid. We mention it here again, if only in passing, because

it is such a telling piece of evidence. Some archaeologists insist the structure is manmade, while most insist they are not, but natural formations. I personally think they are, in large part, natural.

However, as a caveat to this, many archaeologists do admit there is definitely an "artificial influence" involved with them, because there is clear evidence of the stone having been worked by someone having altered this natural pyramid formation. For this to have been accomplished, whoever did this changing of the natural stone structure had to have access to it.

Currently, the pyramid is under as much as 42.7 meters of seawater. So this work had to be done when the sea levels were lower. This would mean the work had to have been done around 10,000 years ago, at least, and probably earlier. Again, this is long before our current civilization even thought of starting, and even before the small "agrarian" settlements existed for millennia prior to the start of our civilization.

5. **Pyramids Around The World.** Pyramids can be found around the world, in China, Egypt, the Canary Islands, Greece, Italy, Southern Bosnia, Mongolia, and more, and these date back as much as 5000 to 8000 years ago, or as some researchers insist, even more. There are also pyramids to be found on Taiwan, the Mauritius Islands, and Tahiti. We will discuss these later on in a little more depth.

6. **Ancient Mines Around The World.** A 40,000 year-old mine has been discovered in South Africa. Some researchers think the mine might even be far older than that. In Australia, a mine dating back 30,000 years has been discovered. In Greece, there is a mine, which it is claimed is at least 15,000 years old. In Northern Chile, a 12,000 year-old mine has been uncovered. Obviously, all these mines around the world predate the rise of civilization by an incredible amount of time, many millennia, in fact. These mines and others of such ancient vintage were to extract a variety of types of metal. Some were to obtain iron

or iron oxide; others were for copper, as well as tin, and even gold. An alloy of copper and tin (among other metals used with the copper) makes bronze, but the Bronze Age, according to most archaeologists, didn't start until around 3300 BCE, and this was the early Bronze Age. Yet, thousands upon thousands of years prior to this, these metals were mined, it seems.

7. **Ancient Michigan "Stonehenge:"** Explorers and researchers have found "monument" stones some 12.2 meters under Lake Michigan. These stones, some arranged in a circle, or "cromlech" as some refer to them, as with Stonehenge of England, were found while the people were looking for old shipwrecks. Estimates are that the stones could be 10,000 years old, or perhaps even older. One monument appears to have the image of a mastodon carved into it. Michigan does have other stone monuments on land, as well as these underwater ones. Considering the depth they are at, they had to have been put there at least 10,000 years ago, and again, probably more if they had once been on dry land.

8. **Baalbek Platform and Temple of the Mount.** The Baalbek platform in Lebanon is old, extremely old. This huge stone platform was originally thought to date back to the time of ancient Rome. Since then, historians have determined that it is much older.

Just how old is unknown. We simply don't know who built it. There is some evidence that the Canaanites had temples built there at one time. This pushes the date of the platform back by more than 2000 years earlier than when the Greeks, and then the Romans, later used it, at least. However, archaeologists are certain the Canaanites were incapable of building something on such a massive scale. They think someone else had to have accomplished this almost miraculous feat. The question is, who?

We do know the location is mentioned in the ancient Sumerian *Epic of Gilgamesh*. In this poem/story, he describes the place as a special platform where great things thundered up and down from heaven, leaving smoke and fire, with the sound of roaring thunder in their wake.

The sheer size of the foundation of these platforms is astonishing, with the Baalbek Platform being the most impressive. Stones, some weighing sometimes more than 1500 tons, were used to build the platform.

Even today, this would be an incredible engineering feat to accomplish. Why? Because some of the stones are so heavy, modern-day workers couldn't fit enough cranes around one of them to lift it. Therefore, just how whoever built the platform of Baalbek did it, is a mystery.

As for the true age of the structure, again we have a problem with dating things made of stone. However, if the platform really was there in the time of that warrior, Gilgamesh, then it is very old indeed. Some suggest it may go back 18,000 to 20,000 years or perhaps even longer.

The Temple Mount in Jerusalem is a sister platform to the one in Baalbek. Its dimensions, though not quite as impressive as those of Baalbek, are still huge. Like Baalbek, a succession of civilizations has built different things on top of that vast platform of stone.

Currently, the Muslim mosque, the Dome of the Rock, is situated there. Jewish history says that both temples, Herod's and Solomon's, were also there. However, like Baalbek, the platform seems to have been there far longer than those temples. This, again, places it in very ancient times. Many researchers surmise that both the Baalbek and Temple of the Mount platforms were built at or near the same time, and predate any known civilization. In addition, as with Baalbek, nobody knows who the builders of these platforms were.

9. **Göbekli Tepe.** In the southern region of Anatolia, Turkey, atop a mountain is a strange place, indeed. Some archaeologists believe the site had religious significance, and that it was used around 8000 BCE. The place also seems to have been used for thousands of years earlier, with some archaeologists saying it dates back to 10,000 BCE. At least 12,000 years old,

with many researchers contending it is much older, Göbekli Tepe is an enigma. There are stone columns, approximately six meters (twenty feet) in height. These pillars were then set into carved-out wells in the bedrock to support them in an upright position. On average, the stones weigh about twenty tons apiece. The columns are in a series of circles. On some of them are carved animals, some of which are not native to anywhere in the region of the Göbekli Tepe site, but rather inhabit regions a vast distance from there. Nobody can account for how such primitive humans, supposedly relatively limited in their travels, could know of such creatures.

For this reason, some think Göbekli Tepe gave rise to the idea of the Garden of Eden, and/or the idea of the Great Flood of Noah. This site has seen long-term use, with some of the structures being much more modern than the most ancient ones.

However, one thing archaeologists do know is that the whole area seems to have been deliberately buried, as if to protect it for some reason. Someone spent a great deal of time and effort moving tons upon tons of earth to bury all these monuments. Again, why anyone would do this is just yet one more enigma of the site. Göbekli Tepe is like so many other stone monuments around the world, a complete mystery.

10. Circular Ruins Around The World. Ruins, some say as much as 200,000 years old, are all over Southern Africa. Some mainstream archaeologists insist these circles are not that old, and were merely a primitive sort of corral system for cattle. This premise (with no real evidence to support it at all), would seem to be in error. Many of the stone circles are closed—no gates. It would be rather hard to let the cattle in and out every day to graze by having to move a bunch of boulders out of the way all the time. There is another issue, as well. The circles seem to have features that are suggestive of being astronomical in nature. Moreover, these so-called "corrals" abound! There are an incredible number of them. Did primitive humanity have that many cattle to keep? Nor is this just in Southern Africa.

11. Circular Ruins in Saudi Arabia, Syria, and Jordan. Satellite imagery has shown large numbers of very similar circular stone enclosures not only in Saudi Arabia, but also in areas of Syria and Jordan, as well. As with the ones in South Africa, nobody knows what culture made these, and being stone, they are impossible to date. Strangely, no artifacts have been found in or near the stone circles to suggest they are burial sites, corrals (no bones of any cattle, desiccated feces, etc, found), or even dwellings. Just what they are, and what their true age is, is still a mystery. However, judging by other events, natural landscape erosion of geographical features around the ones in South Africa, etc, some researchers and archaeologists think they may be truly ancient, and by that, we mean hundreds of thousands of years, rather than just thousands or even tens of thousands of years. Researcher, Michael Tellinger, makes a compelling case for the stones having certain special acoustical properties, as well, although to date, I have not been able to verify this as being accurate or not.

12. Circular Ruins In Peru. Remember, earlier I mentioned evidence had to be global in nature to help prove a worldwide civilization? Well, here we have more circular structures, and this time in Peru, South America. Again, no one is sure who built them. However, they look astonishingly similar to the stone circles of South Africa and the Middle East. Just what their use was, is also a matter of purest conjecture. Nobody seems really to know. Although archaeologists think they are only a matter of a millennium or two old, again, they have no way of knowing for sure.

A lack of stone implements around them, or anything to indicate their use, leaves their function and age a mystery. Without such corroborating finds, it makes it very hard to tell the age of the structures. Once more, many researchers think the structures date back far earlier than the time the archaeologists are saying, and point to the fact that such stone circles do not seem to have been a part of the Native American civilizations of those times. In fact, the descendants of those peoples claimed they never built such structures. They insist "others" built them.

13. Stones Of Carnac. These stone monuments, or "menhirs" as some refer to such stones, in France are incredible. There are over 3000 individual stone monuments. They were erected over a long duration, and archaeologists think some were raised as early as 4500 BCE. Again, other researchers question this and say that some of them date back far earlier than even this. They point to a series of stones on an island close to shore near there. The line of stones is incomplete, since a portion of the stones is submerged under the water. They point out that this means the stones had been placed there further back in time then archaeologists claim, because it had to be when the sea levels were much lower.

Many of the stones, although very weathered, do seem to have the faint outlines of having been carved or engraved with the shapes of people. The stones are set in straight lines for the most part and go on for kilometers. Just what the purpose for erecting so many stones was, is hard to say. Again, most archaeologists contend they were for religious and/or astronomical reasons. Still, nobody seems to know for sure. Nevertheless, the effort involved, as well as the time involved, was incredible. How supposedly tiny agricultural settlements with their limited resources and capabilities could accomplish such improbably difficult structures is a complete mystery. We seem to have many of them.

14. Adam's Calendar. The so-called Adam's Calendar may well be the world's oldest Megalithic site, since by some estimates it is thought to be at least 75,000 years old! This is, as usual, subject to some debate, but that it predates all other known megalithic structures seems a certainty. Adam's Calendar is older than the Pyramids of Giza, Stonehenge, Carnac, and more.

This "African Stonehenge" is located in South Africa and is a circular series of stones, with other stones placed inside of it. Some thirty meters in diameter, the Adam's Calendar also has stones aligned in such a way that, like the Stonehenge of England, they appear to create some type of calendar. There seem to be alignments with the star constellation of Orion, which if accurate, dates the site back to 11,500 BCE or more. The calendar is located near Mpumalanga and the stones' weight, on average, is around five tons each.

However, further calculations have been done. If one takes into consideration the stones may have aligned with all three stars of Orion, instead of just the one, then the stones may be as old as 160,000 years. This is not just based on the Orion Constellation rising on the "flat horizon" as one researcher put it, but also on the apparent erosion, that has taken place on all the stones of the circle.

This area we referred to earlier as having stone circles similar as in the Middle East, and Peru, but Adam's Calendar is by far and away the most complete "calendar" of such an antiquated age in the entire area of South Africa, if not everywhere. Estimates of the other types of circles say there are no less than 100,000 of them in total! There is no way all of these could have been just some type of corral system. There would have to have been hundreds of thousands of cattle to fill them all.

Moreover, even among this many stone circles, Adam's Calendar is considered unique. One final note; as with the other stone circles, this area seems to have been very popular for gold mining with various mines and shafts spotted not far from Adam's Calendar. Some of these mines date back tens of thousands of years, according to some researchers.

15. Spiral Design. Spirals—how they abound around the planet! Virtually every culture seems to have incorporated them someway. From ancient rock petroglyphs to tombs and more, the spiral is probably the most commonly recurring image of ancient cultures worldwide. Egypt, Greece, Sumeria, Babylon, Neolithic cultures, even the Native Americans use the spiral.

Usually, the design represents that which is sacred in some way.

When considering there may have once been a planet-wide written language, one that used strange hieroglyphics similar to those of Egypt, as we will later discuss, it is of interest to note there also seems to be a particular use of certain designs, as well. This isn't just true of the ubiquitous spiral, but other designs, as well.

16. The Swastika. I end this section with a brief discussion about the swastika, yet another design that seems to have proliferated in ancient times and worldwide. Yes, again, these days, we all equate that symbol with the hated German Nazi regime of World War II, and Adolph Hitler's hideous Nazi Party, but the swastika is a far old symbol than just being that of the Third Reich, as in Arkaim, Russia.

The swastika dates back thousands of years and is found in cultures and their drawings, including pictographs and petroglyphs in various places around the world, especially in the northern hemisphere. Native American tribes have used the swastika, as have the ancient Hindus of India, and others. There is no other way to put it; the swastika was an immensely popular symbol, and often used as a positive one, more often than not having strong religious connotations. It was left to the Nazis of the twentieth century to pervert the meaning of the symbol to something truly dark. How old is the swastika thought to be? Well, it seems to date back to about 12,000 years, or possibly more. This puts it right around 10,000 BCE, a date we will keep seeing more of here.

The purpose of this chapter wasn't to bore the reader to death with an endless series of things they may have already read about in the way of stone monuments. Rather it was to point out some very important issues:

1. There are incredible structures, massive ones, dating far back in time, past the supposed beginning of civilization in

3500 BCE. That our civilization erupted "almost overnight," and "exploded" as archaeologists put it, seems to be without question. Nevertheless, this explosion of civilization didn't occur much before 3500 BCE. Therefore, by archaeologists' own definition of what existed prior to civilization, these mammoth stone objects shouldn't have been built. Furthermore, nobody can account for how they were built by such primitive peoples, and in many cases, thousands upon thousands of years before the rise of modern civilization. Some questions that arise are:

a. How could tiny agrarian settlements have the work force to create such huge monuments carved in stone?

b. How could such rudimentary villages come up with the resources to create such things as the Baalbek platform? It would seem fundamentally impossible such isolated and tiny communities could do such a thing.

c. Where did the expertise come from to create such "monumental" structures? We're talking about structures that even today would be unbelievably difficult to build in many cases. Yet, we are supposed to believe that rudimentary settlements of perhaps twenty-five to a couple of hundred people at most, are capable of creating such edifices? It would seem manifestly unlikely, and it is even more unbelievable.

d. Why would such tiny and isolated groups of individuals struggle so to build these things? What was their true purpose? Nobody seems to know.

2. We have shown by the locations of many of these stone monuments that they didn't exist in just one region at about the same time, but apparently, were worldwide in nature. The similarity of the structures is also hard not to see. Stone circles, upright monuments, and all of carved rock strongly suggest that not only was the knowledge of how to do such things worldwide, but that it might have come from one source.

In any case, wherever the knowledge came from, it seems to have disseminated on a worldwide basis.

3. The age of building such stone monuments came to an abrupt end; it seems, with no more built after that time. Around the world, construction of such monuments ended.

This was the point of this chapter, to show that almost all the stone monuments all date far back in time, and long before the rise of our current civilization. In any case, here we have our first clues, hard evidence (in stone) of a worldwide civilization, and the fact that our timeline of civilization seems to stretch much further back in time than most archaeologists claim. There are more clues to be found. Moreover, I think what they lead to is amazing.

Nevertheless, our puzzle is far from over. In fact, it has just begun. We need many more pieces of the puzzle yet, to come to an idea of what our final jigsaw-puzzle picture will look like. Do we have such pieces? Oh, yes. It would seem we do.

Having made our first efforts to establish that civilization goes much further back than archaeologists think, and this this was worldwide and not just limited to any one region, we need to move on. However, let us remember, we have our first major hallmarks of a worldwide civilization. The culture used stone for their constructions and these structures often had astronomical links, with the constellation of Orion often prominently figuring into it all, as we shall also see later on in this book. Now for our next pieces of the puzzle...

CHAPTER 4

AN UNDERGROUND WORLD

At this point, we are well underway in establishing our timeline. On that long line of world history, we have placed the beginning of modern civilization at 3500 BCE. However, by using stone monuments found around the world, we also know that some sort of civilization, one of seemingly great capabilities existed at some time much longer ago.

This, judging by all the varying locations of stone monuments found, would seem to have been a global one. No continent is without its stone monuments and/or petroglyphs, and other signs of a very ancient culture. By ancient, we mean a civilization that dates back 12,000 years. So we must conclude that such a worldwide civilization must have existed, since we have hard evidence for it.

We must also conclude that archaeologists in the mainstream have it wrong in this regard. Either that or all these stone monuments around the world shouldn't exist at all. Remember, that although there undoubtedly were many tiny agrarian settlements scattered around the globe, along with tribes of hunter-gatherers roaming as nomads everywhere, these people could not have created all these colossal monuments. The evidence is against this. Archaeologists themselves say they didn't have the capabilities.

Furthermore, isolated communities, as archaeologists refer to them, by the very definition of isolated, could not have been in contact with each other around the planet. Therefore, such tiny communities could not dispense the knowledge of building stone monuments on a global or even larger regional basis. Again, this is by mainstream archaeologists' description of the world at the time.

So if not our primitive humans being ultimately responsible for such things, then who did build all the stone monuments? Who built Göbekli Tepe? Who built Carnac with its thousands upon thousands of stone monuments? Who did it so long ago that now the sea covers part of those monuments? Once more, it hardly seems feasible a few nascent farmers could manage all this.

There are more oddities and pieces of the timeline puzzle and they are worldwide in nature, too. For example, we have the strange problem of what amounts to an underground world. All around the Earth, there are caves, caverns, and tunnel systems, for which we simply can't account. Many of these are manmade, or at least artificial. Again, we have no idea of when they were made or why. Neither do we know who built them. Let's take a quick look at just some examples of this phenomenon:

1. **Underground Tunnel Discovered Between Sicily And Calabria.** Last year, in 2014, rumors spread of the discovery of an underground tunnel under the Strait of Messina. It is said the tunnel must've been built shortly after the era of the Punic wars. This puts it in ancient Roman times. However, there is a problem with that theory. The tunnel would have had to run so deeply, that there would have been issue with the Romans who tried to dig it. These problems would include, but not be limited to, suffering from the "bends," or decompression sickness.

Furthermore, although the Romans were master engineers, their technology, like all modern technologies, had to develop over time. Therefore, it is unlikely that so far in their past they were capable of such a fantastic feat of engineering. Besides, there is no record of any such tunnel ever having been built, and like the Chinese, the Romans kept copious records of everything.

Surely, such an incredible endeavor would have been recorded in some fashion or other. After all, such a tunnel would have been far more difficult than building Hadrian's Wall, for example. The tunnel upon completion would have been celebrated, made much of. So new is this information that it is still hotly debated whether this is a hoax or not. Then all discoveries always go through such a debate, it seems. Anything that deviates from the expected results in mainstream archaeology always faces major hurdles. Yet, to date, the evidence seems to indicate that such a tunnel might have existed. If so, it is doubtful the Romans built it and the more probable scenario is the tunnel is much older, had been there long before the Romans.

2. **Tunnels In Europe.** Extensive tunnels have been discovered dating back 12,000 years or more. These tunnels are below hundreds, if not thousands of Neolithic sites. The tunnels are large and can be anywhere from 700 meters to as little as 350 meters. The longest is in Germany and the shortest is in Austria. However, the tunnels are not restricted to these two regions, but have been found all over Europe, including even Scotland. Considering that these tunnels have all existed for so many millennia without collapsing, it should be pointed out that despite being a so-called "stone age" people, their ability to excavate such tunnels was very good, seemingly too good.

Just what tools they used is something of a mystery, though, as is the purpose of the tunnels themselves, but some archaeologists believe they were used to get around safely below the earth's surface. Just how these tunnels might have helped in this regard is a bit of a puzzle, because surely, if they could dig these, they could build aboveground structures for safety, just as easily, or even more so. Additionally, they wouldn't provide much safety from other people of the period if they all used such tunnels and so all knew about them. In fact, there is nothing to show they were used in a defensive way at all.

3. **Longyou Caves.** In China, located on Phoenix Hill in Zhejiang
   province there are a series of caves. These caves are artificial,
   meaning they were manmade. They are referred to, collectively,
   as the Longyou Caves. These were discovered in 1992. So far,
   some twenty-four caves have been revealed.

The caves were excavated in an area that is largely composed
of siltstone. All archaeologists can say about them is they were
created some time before to 1200 BCE. This was before the Qin
Dynasty took power. The odd thing about these caves is they don't
connect, although they are close together. It is as if each was
supposed to be a separate sealed pocket. If so, these were large
pockets, indeed. The sheer scale of them, of their construction
must have been a truly daunting task. The caves, carved from
solid rock, make it impossible to know their real age. There are no
implements left behind, nothing in the way of artifacts of any kind
to indicate who built them, when, or why. Therefore, their true age
is a matter of conjecture.

Yet, the work involved was enormous. Putting aside the
arduous task of excavating thousands and thousands of tons of
rock and debris to accomplish this task, there is the matter of
how finished the carving of the caverns is. They contain columns
and pillars. One can only describe them as having been done in
an intricate way. Not only the floor, but the ceiling and columns,
as well, have thousands of parallel grooves etched in them. These
are so precise, so consistent, it is hard to imagine stonemasons
accomplishing such a feat, yet somehow they did. Moreover, why
they would bother doing this to the ceilings, as well, is a matter of
some debate.

However, the patterns are markedly the same as those seen on
800 BCE pottery, which might or might not help in determining the
age of the caves, since this may have been a chance coincidence,
or the pottery markings may have come from the markings in the
cave, and so the caves are older. Nobody is sure.

Finally, there are mysterious reports that the caves, seven in
total, were dug in a pattern to mimic, below ground, the Orion
Constellation above them in the sky. As mentioned, this, too,

seems a recurring theme in ancient sites for monuments, since it is established the Pyramids of Giza were laid out in the same pattern, as were other monuments around the world of the times. For some reason, still unknown, the Orion Constellation figures prominently in many ancient cultures around the world. Why this should be so is an enigma.

Furthermore, there is no historical evidence for these caves existing. The ancient Chinese kept meticulous records, copious amounts of them and of just about everything, but nothing in any of the records refers to these caves. It was as if they were meant to be anonymous, or done long before such records were kept. More to the point, they had to have been done so long ago that even human memory of them vanished completely. There aren't even any legends or myths of anyone having built such caverns or caves in the area, no folklores, and no stories handed down.

Another curious point about these caverns is that there is no sign of what they were used for. Again, there are no religious artifacts, sculptures, or carvings of any sort within them. There is no debris of any sort, as of people having lived there, or even having stayed there for a while. The places are clean. This is frustrating in the extreme, since we can't know what purpose the caverns had without finding such things.

When we say the caves are large, they are. The floor area of one cave, as an example, is over a 1000 square meters in size. The interior height of some of the caves can reach as high as thirty meters. What's more, combined, the caves cover a total area of more than 30,000 meters! Yet once more, there is no record of who built them, why, or when. This, in itself, is very strange.

I have to refer back to the fact that the caves are isolated from each other, with no interconnecting tunnels passageways. This signifies the caves were supposed to be separate, and must have been made so for a very specific reason. What might that reason have been? We'll get to that later on.

4. **Underground City In Turkey.** Last year, in Turkey, the government announced they had discovered a huge underground city. This was not the one already known. This subterranean city

is located in the Cappadocia area of Anatolia, Turkey. After excavation, archaeologists were amazed to find an incredible complex of rooms, tunnels, passageways, chambers, and "open" spaces. This was an undertaking on a vast scale.

Mainstream archaeologists date the city to around the time of 3000 BCE, or right near the beginning of modern civilization. However, since it is a place carved from rock and earth, it is impossible to estimate the true age of this underground city. That different people inhabited it at different times seems likely, because of artifacts found there.

Still, at the very least, the city dates back 5000 years. We are also talking about a city on a truly large scale. For instance, the tunnels are kilometers long, and some are wide enough to drive a vehicle through them. The question is, why were these people underground? What drove them to forsake the surface of the Earth for a place they must've felt was safer, despite frequent earthquakes in the region? In addition, why such wide tunnels at a time when the wheel had not yet been invented?

5. **Grand Canyon Mystery.** In the New World, we have our own tales of underground cities and tunnels, as well as strange caverns. Such is the case of the Grand Canyon. These stories date back a long ways. For instance, there's the strange tale about a cave at the base of the Grand Canyon. This appeared on April 5, 1909 in the *Phoenix Gazette*. The headline read: "Explorations In Grand Canyon." The article mentions a man by the name of G.E. Kinkaid. The Smithsonian Institute purportedly funded his expedition.

While exploring in a narrow ravine of the Grand Canyon, he claimed to have discovered a cave, or more rightly, a small complex of them. He said there was a central chamber from which tunnels radiated outward "like spokes of a wheel," as he put it. He estimated the chamber to be some 457.2 meters underground.

In the tunnels, he stated there were hundreds of chambers. These, like some vast museum, held such things as archaic weapons, implements made of copper, and other items that had never been in use by Native Americans. He also claimed to have discovered a chamber with what looked to be male mummies. These were shrouded in a type of fabric, which he thought might have been made from bark.

Mr. Kinkaid also saw what he described as a sort of "shrine," with a seated, cross-legged idol, reminiscent of Buddha. The idol held lotus blossoms. He also claimed there were plaques or tablets with hieroglyphics on them, reminiscent of ancient Egyptian hieroglyphics.

In short, the cavern, with its massive main chamber, many radiating "spokes," and smaller rooms, each filled with artifacts of various sorts, seemed to be designed as a repository, a safe place to hold the incredible contents.

Was this a hoax? Attempts to find the cavern now have met with negative results, so it is certainly possible. However, not all of the Grand Canyon's twists and turns, its many side canyons and ravines have been explored as yet. Furthermore, there seems to have been little point in perpetrating such a hoax, nothing to be gained from such a thing.

In 1909, Phoenix, Arizona was little more than a town in size, so the audience would have been very small for such a hoax. Moreover, report after report of underground caverns, tunnels, ancient ones, have been made over the last few centuries, and some of those certainly are real. The *Phoenix Gazette* was definitely not known for any sort of sensationalism, or tabloid type journalism. Quite the opposite, in fact. The newspaper had a history of being conservative and careful in its reporting. Furthermore, there really are caves in the Grand Canyon, some with entrances that do not look "natural."

As an interesting side note, the Hopi Native Americans have long held the belief that they emerged from underground caverns in the region of the Grand Canyon and that the "Ant People" had protected them in those caves until such time as it was safe for them to come to the surface. We will refer back to this idea later on.

At this point, I need to mention that many of these "cave" or "cavern" stories all seem to relate in some way or other to people trying to find a safe refuge, a place below the surface where they might better survive. Either that or the caves seemed to have been used for some other purpose, such as repositories of knowledge or such use.

In conclusion, we can only say the number of stories about the caverns, strange chambers filled with marvelous and exotic artifacts, is in the thousands. There are tales from around the world of people having chanced upon such finds in such places as North and South America, Europe, Africa, and Asia. Always the stories seem to have a similar theme. Hidden chambers well below the Earth's surface, tunnels, and/or stone corridors that lead to not only strange repositories of artifacts, but often to encounters with strange beings. These people are often taller than normal humans, and by far. In Arkansas, one such story tells of finding such people. They told their discoverers they were direct descendants of Noah.

How do we account for literally thousands of such stories by so many different people? Why is it we can find caverns of such a nature, such as the ones in China? Why does nobody there have any knowledge, any historical record of something engineered on such a grand scale?

The bizarre thing is that often, there aren't even local legends or myths with regard to such things, as is the case of the caves in China. It is as if the very existence of such places is lost to the racial memory of the locals there. In addition, why is there so much of this underground connection? Whatever it is, whatever the reason, the finds and the stories are worldwide in nature.

Again, we have another mysterious piece of the puzzle, and this one, like all the others, exists on a global scale. Are some tales fiction? Almost certainly, this is so. Still the number of real caves, caverns, and tunnels are in such huge numbers, that something seems to have been going on long ago. People at one time, it seemed, saw such places as sanctuaries, or places to store what was important to them, as in their heritage. So the next question that must be asked is why? Why did they feel the need to do this? What danger were they facing that they felt the need to preserve either their own lives, or that of their culture? Being worldwide, it must have been something big.

CHAPTER 5

OOPART

Having established someone was building stone monuments around the world for thousands of years before the beginning of current civilization, can we find any other evidence for a civilization, a worldwide one, having existed prior to ours? Yes, and in a number of ways. One of them is with something referred to as "oopart." A silly name because, I suppose, many archaeologists thought it was a silly subject. However, it's more of an extraordinary subject, because after investigating this phenomenon, there does seem to be real evidence to support the fact many of these "oopart" items are genuine.

What is oopart? Well, the term refers to any objects of an anomalous nature, and ones that shouldn't be where they are found. An anachronism is another name for such a thing.

When we talk about oopart, we're talking about actual objects found either in archaeological sites, or in layers of rock or sediment where they simply shouldn't be. Archaeologists, mainstream ones, find this a very difficult thing to believe in. This is, perhaps, because they have so much of their time, careers, and livelihood invested in the idea that oopart simply can't be, shouldn't exist.

Therefore, they either put such discoveries down as:

1. Being a hoax,

2. Being a "mistake," or...

3. They just ignore the matter entirely and refuse to comment on such discoveries at all. This last is that denial thing rearing its ugly head again. Sadly, denial of something doesn't mean that "something" will just go away. Although, I'm sure many archaeologists would like that to happen.

So what are examples of oopart? Well, here are some:

1. **Sunken Great Pyramids of Giza.** In an article published by Paul Darin on March 6, 2015 in the *Epoch Times*, he talks about an archaeologist who makes a startling claim. Sherif El Morsi, the archaeologist in question, has a long history of delving into the secrets of the Giza Pyramids, the Sphinx, and the whole area of the Giza plateau. He has spent over twenty years researching all this.

Sherif El Morsi claims the sea had to have inundated the area, but after the pyramids and Sphinx were already there. To support his claim, he mentions a fossil of a sea urchin embedded in the surface stone. He stated this in a paper he and Antoine Gigal— another investigator of the Giza Pyramids and Sphinx—published. If the area had seawater at one time, this would make the Sphinx and the pyramids far older than originally thought.

Nor are Sherif El Morsi and Antoine Gigal alone in this belief. Doctor Robert M. Schloch, over a decade ago, pointed to the fact water erosion patterns on the Sphinx seemed older than believed, as well. He placed the probable age of the Sphinx from 5000 BCE to 9000 BCE. The lower number would make the Sphinx 7000 years old and the higher number would make it 11,000 years old.

The fossil of the sea urchin was discovered on a block of limestone of the temple, and this is used as proof the sea had to have made incursions there at one time in the past. Other archaeologists argue this is a mistake. They say the fossil is just another of many such fossils to be found in limestone.

However, in direct contradiction to this, Archaeologist Sherif El Morsi says that:

a. The fossil is much larger than the microfossils normally found in such limestone.

b. The fossil was lying flat, as it would if the creature had planted itself there on the surface of the block, as sea urchins do.

c. Sherif also points to the "pristine" condition of the sea urchin fossil. If the fossil had been exposed to the elements due to erosion of the limestone block, it would have shown marks of erosion, as well. The thing does not. Archaeologist Sherif El Morsi doesn't believe it is a fossil in the sense of one dating back millions of years in the limestone, but underwent a much swifter process by being filled with wet sediments. This, too, would also account for its "pristine" condition.

Based on this, Archaeologist Sherif El Morsi claims the whole plateau area has been the victim of some type of rising sea level or sea surge. This wouldn't have been a deep submersion, but more in the nature of a large shallow area. However, the waters were deep enough to submerge the Sphinx, as well as other structures, although probably not the pyramids themselves, at least not completely. He claims this created a new shoreline. This wave-lapping action resulted in erosion of the stones in the area due to "tidal ebbing."

Was the Giza Plateau inundated at one time? Was there a sea surge, one that lasted long enough for sea urchins to embed themselves on the rocks of some of the temples? There is a hot debate raging over this issue. Noted archaeologists on both sides of the argument are vehement about what they "believe" to be true. Nobody knows for sure, at least, not yet.

However, there does seem to be some real evidence for the plateau having been flooded. There also seems to be evidence for the Pyramids and the Sphinx being older than is claimed by most archaeologists. Moreover, other archaeologists champion Sherif El Morsi's claims, as well.

2. **30,000 BCE. Stone with Engravings Uncovered in China**. A stone, which Chinese archaeologists insist goes back some 30,000 years, and with engravings on it, was found in a collection of primitive stone tools. This was at the Shuidonggou Palaeolithic site, which was undergoing excavation in 1980. The stone appears to have been used as a method for counting, for the markings are only made once, with no repetitions. The significance of this find cannot be underestimated. Someone, 30,000 years ago, was making marks on the stone that imply a method of counting long before this was believed to have happened, and by tens of thousands of years.

3. **The Nimrud Lens.** In the Palace of Nimrud archaeologists unearthed something very strange, indeed. This was a lens. Photos of it show it is round, and very lens-like in shape and apparent function. It seems this lens was used as part of a telescope. If so, this is astounding, that a telescope existed 3000 years ago. Here in the West, we think of Galileo as introducing the telescope, and this occurred just a few centuries ago.

4. **Infamous Piri Reis Map.** Now, I'm sure you have heard of the Piri Reis Map before, but I'd be remiss not saying something about it for those who might not have heard of it, and just how in particular it pertains to our puzzle here. The year was 1929 and a discovery was made of a map, one printed on a hide, no less.

Historians, after initially thinking the map was a forgery, discovered it was, in fact, authentic. Just a minimal amount of research was needed to discover the fact the map belonged to an admiral of the Turkish fleet. This was in the 1500s. He had a predilection for maps and this map, the Piri Reis Map, named for him, is thought to be an assembly of several other maps he had access to. Some of the maps used to create his compilation dated back to around 400 BCE, and some of these were said to have been copies of even earlier maps.

So far, this is no big deal. The problem comes when one actually looks at the map. Remember, this chart was compiled by Piri Reis in the 1500s and the world had not yet been completely explored. Australia and Antarctica, for instance, had not yet been discovered.

However, the Piri Reis map shows not only the Atlantic coastline of Africa and South America, but oddly, the coastline of Antarctica, as well. This mapping of the northern coastline of Antarctica is not just a vague outline, but replete with many particulars. Moreover, the map shows features that have been buried on a thick layer of ice for what some geologists say has to have been for at least the last million years! The exact amount of time is argued, but that it is a very long time indeed, is not in question.

However long the ice has been there, the mapping of Antarctica is still some three hundred years, at a minimum, before the continent was supposed to have even been discovered. Additionally, the latest possible date Queen Maud Land could have been charted in an ice-free state is around 4000 BCE. This is according to one expert. There are problems with even this claim. Most other geologists insist the ice sheet and ice shelf has been there for no less than millions of years!

No matter what figures one uses, the numbers still don't work out. Antarctica, it seems, was known by someone at a time when there was no ice on it's northern coast. This means, and as various researchers claim, the earliest the map could have been drawn in such detail had to have been around 9000 BCE or even far earlier. Therefore, at a minimum, the map, or at least the map used to help create the Piri Reis Map, is around 11,000 years old, and probably more.

No known civilization, at least none known to mainstream archaeologists had the technology or the capability of creating such charts, nor do the records of any later civilizations in any way refer to the existence of Antarctica. However, if there had been the civilization of Atlantis around that time, then of course, a map of the entire Atlantic region, from continent to continent (Africa to South America), and down to the Antarctic doesn't seem at all a farfetched idea, but rather a practical measure. Surely, those living in Atlantis, if it was situated in the Atlantic, would map the areas around them, including the Americas, Europe, Africa, and Antarctica?

Again, no matter how one prefers to view the Piri Reis Map, and it has been proven authentic, one simply cannot account for an ice-free Antarctica, or even any sort of map of Antarctic at all through the normal means of history or archaeology. The map is a complete enigma in this regard.

5. **Pyramid With The Eye.** Found in Ecuador, the Pyramid of the Eye is not a large stone, but it is unique. The eye of this little pyramid is inlaid, not part of the original stone, and it is quite intricate. Many say it does not look like an animal's eye, but that neither does it look human. There are thirteen levels to the pyramid, layers of etched "blocks." The astonishing thing about this stone is that it looks exactly like the pyramid with the eye at the top of it as seen on the US dollar. The resemblance is truly uncanny.

The base upon which the pyramid sits has tiny gold circular areas on it. These are arranged in the pattern of the constellation of Orion. (We see this cropping up of the Orion stars yet again.) This is significant, because many researchers say the exact same thing is true of the Egyptian Pyramids of Giza and that, seen from above, they, too, are exactly arranged in the same pattern of the Orion constellation. Even the nearby Nile River mirrors the river of stars that crosses the night sky known as the Milky Way. So, on two widely separated continents, we have these incredible similarities.

There is also a strange form of what appears to be a type of hieroglyphic writing on the bottom of the pyramid, as well. Furthermore, these strange markings are seen elsewhere, in other places around the world. Doctor Kurt Schildmann, former

President of the German Linguistic Association, claims the writing appears to be a type of "Pre-Sanskrit," supposedly the oldest known written language on Earth. This miniature pyramid was found close to the site of the discovery of the World Stone Map, which we will discuss a little later on.

Furthermore, other stones and objects from around the world show these similar sorts of markings, or type of writing. Whatever they mean, they appear to have been disseminated on a worldwide basis.

6. **Metal Pipes of Baigong Cave.** Here, we have another cave in China. This one is unusual in that it contained metal pipes, as a number of researchers refer to these strange objects. Some archaeologists claim they are not metal pipes at all, but rather fossilized tree roots that ran down to the nearby lake. Yet, this explanation is unsatisfactory, for such archaeologists can't explain the metallic nature of these "pipes." Furthermore, no one can explain the reason for the pipes' existence. Therefore, exactly what these pipes are, or what they were used for, is still a mystery. Still, some conjecture that rather than being tree roots, they were, indeed, pipes, and were used to bring water up from the lake.

7. **Very Old Oopart Artifacts.** Among these sorts of artifacts are some very strange ones. What makes them so bizarre is not so much what they are, but because of how old they appear to be. These objects are often dug up from the earth and found embedded in layers of coal or rock. They often are only discovered when the rock or lumps of coal are cracked open. This means they have to be hundreds of thousands, or even millions, of years old.

Again, the word "hoax" is often used, but considering this has been going on for a several centuries now, it's hard to believe these are all hoaxes in their thousands. These objects have been found around the world, at different times. In most cases, these objects have not been tampered with and when discovered, are still firmly embedded in the surrounding matrix of stone. Most archaeologists can't say how such a situation could come about, and rather than attempt to discover the answer, they won't even consider such finds. They choose, rather, simply to ignore them. To date, over 3000 such oopart objects have been discovered!

8. **The Lanzhou Stone.** Here is a much more recently discovered object. It is referred to as the Lanzhou Stone. It is a rock in which is embedded a "threaded" metal bar. Zhilin Wang in the Marzong Mountain area of China discovered this. The stone is unfamiliar to researchers. More to the point, no one seems to know what type of stone it is. This makes for much conjecture that it might be a meteorite, but there have been no tests conducted to confirm this idea. Therefore, it is just a supposition.

And if this is a hoax, it is a truly incredible one. The rock has been examined by the best experts China has on the subject, which include geologists, and even a physicist. They could arrive at no conclusions other than the metal, a threaded metal bar, was firmly embedded in the center of the stone. What's more, all of these researchers pointedly ruled out the possibility of a hoax.

Their conclusion about the stone? Although they believe the artifact of the threaded bar was intelligently made, they can't account for it otherwise. The stone is about 466 grams in weight. The dimensions of the rock are eight centimeters by six centimeters.

9. **Nail Embedded In Rock.** An iron nail was found at the Kingoodie Quarry in Scotland in 1845. Sir David Brewster reported this find to the British Association for the Advancement of Science. His credentials were impeccable. The nail is firmly stuck in the rock. The quarry had been open for some twenty years, so although no one is sure at what layer it was discovered, it can be assumed it was one of the deeper levels. This means it dates far back in time, perhaps millions of years.

10. "Iron Instrument." In 1852, while excavating coal from mines in Scotland, miners came across an "iron instrument." The object in question was embedded in the coal, and nobody was able to find any way it could have been placed there artificially. The "instrument" looks something like a drill bit. There were no openings to suggest that somehow the item has been placed in the center of the piece of coal through such a hole. The only other solution is the coal actually formed around the item. If this is so, then the "instrument" dates back possibly over 100 million years, or more.

11. Rocky Tools. From 1786 through 1788, in the city of Aixen in France, quarrying was done. At a depth of some 15.24 meters, workers came upon a number of strange items. Buried in the sand between two solid layers of rock were the bases of stone columns. Along with these, were the fossilized handles of what seemed to be meant as parts of hammers. Furthermore, the workers found a fossilized wooden board. This was no small piece of fossil, being close to 2.43 meters long and over an .025 meters thick.

The workmen pieced together the various parts, and found they had a quarryman's board. This was incredibly similar to the type of quarryman boards they used. This seemed utterly impossible to them, that someone had been quarrying this area millions of years ago, and using the same type of equipment the quarry men of the eighteenth century were using. As usual, some sounded the cry of "hoax," yet even those naysayers couldn't account for the fact of the fossilized finds. To date, no one has managed to synthesize agate, and so it would appear these fossils are real.

12. The Guadeloupe Woman. Here we have another weird mystery. The skeletal remains of a woman were found. The head and feet were missing but the rest of the skeleton was intact. The skeleton is definitely that of a woman, who must have been, approximately, five foot two in height. Here's the truly weird part; the fossil remains were in a very hard limestone. This layer of limestone has been dated to having been created about twenty-five million years ago. The discovery was made on the coastal shores of Guadalupe Island. This was in 1812, and the island is located in the Caribbean.

Researchers and scientists can't account for the discovery. The idea it was a hoax also seems ludicrous in the extreme. The stone is very hard. The discovery was a genuine one. For some members of the expedition to have stolen off into the dead of night and somehow found the fossilized remains of a woman, and then embedded the remains somehow into the middle of a layer of limestone just isn't plausible. They had neither the tools nor technology.

Remember, this was 1812, after all. People at the time had neither the means nor the method of creating such an elaborate hoax. Then, there is the question of motivation. Nobody had any. After all, it was unlikely scientists of the time would accept such a thing, and anyone who tried to force the issue would have been labeled "crackpots." Therefore, nobody had anything to gain by perpetrating such a hoax, even if they could have, and even if they did have the means or capability, which they most certainly did not.

13. Sky Stones. Objects referred to as "Sky Stones" have been found in Africa. Whatever they are, they do not appear to be a natural material, but rather some artificially combined substance. They are very blue, hence their name. Analysis of the "stones" shows that some contain up to thirteen percent iridium, an element not found on earth at any significant level at all. However, iridium is found in asteroids.

When we find iridium, we rightfully assume there has been an asteroid/meteorite impact of some type. As an example, one of the factors in concluding an asteroid impact in the Yucatan Peninsula wiped out the dinosaurs sixty-five million years ago is a worldwide, geological boundary layer containing iridium. Dinosaurs existed before this layer was laid down, but vanished afterwards. In any case, no one can account for these "sky stones," or say for sure what their origin or use was.

Other Oddities. There are many more such historical oddities. A figurine discovered had a small steel ball inside of it. Mind you, the figurine is dated to be at least 7000 years in age, if not more, and inside this was a metal ball! This, after examination, was discovered to be chromatic steel in composition. Moreover, early x-rays of the statue clearly showed the figurine was sealed. Discovered in 1904, this was a time well before we had chromatic steel. Certainly, humans weren't supposed to have had such a metal, not even any form of steel, seven thousand years ago!

The Iron Age only began around 1200 BCE, just 3200 years or so ago. So how could a steel ball, chromatic steel at that, have existed some 3800 years before the first Iron Age?

Yet more examples of oopart? An iron ladle embedded inside of a large lump of coal was stumbled upon. Sealed inside of the coal, nobody can account for how this could have happened, because the coal was millions of years old.

In conclusion, one must remember all these are just examples. There are many more such oopart artifacts, thousands of them. Everything from ladles embedded inside of chunks of coal, to strange hand-bells also found in coal, as well as cubes of polished aluminum found deep in the ground, we have more such anomalies than we know what to do with.

What does archaeology make of these? Well, the answer to that is simple. Nothing. They make nothing of it. They simply don't talk about it. Apparently, it is easier simply to ignore something that challenges one's whole world viewpoint.

However, as much as they might like it too, archaeologists ignoring the strange historical anomalies don't make them go away. Many are available in museums for one to see, if one wishes. So yes, they are real. But what to make of it all?

Well, several things emerge from studying these ooparts:

1. Historical anomalies definitely do exist. They have for centuries, and so far, around 3000 of them have been discovered.

2. It is unlikely in the extreme that all these anomalies are hoaxes. However, archaeologists simply don't know what to make of them, so they call them that, or don't deal with them at all.

3. Some oopart items show things that just shouldn't be. The World Map Stone is one example. This stone is ancient. Yet, the rock shows a world map. Again, we will discuss this stone more later on.

However, we also have evidence of caves, tunnels, caverns and even underground cities. These subterranean anomalies exist around the world. Many if not most of the tunnels and caves are artificial in nature. But whatever their purpose was, we simply don't know. Even when, how, and why they were built is lost to us.

Moreover, we have evidence of strange markings, very similar ones, from objects around the world. These, too, also date back to 12,000 BCE. or even earlier. They seem to be a form of writing. Furthermore, this "writing" has been found in locations worldwide. From Ecuador to China, there are objects with these markings on them.

So what do we have so far? Well we have evidence of worldwide building, as well as an unknown worldwide written language. We also have global evidence of underground chambers and tunnels, whose purposes are unknown to us. It must also be remembered that some of the so-called oopart objects also seem to date back even millions of years. Even counting the possibility some of these things might be hoaxes perpetrated on scientists of the Twentieth, Ninteenth, and Eighteenth Centuries; this still leaves us with many strange things with which to deal. Certainly, there are far too many simply to ignore them.

The important thing we can gather from this chapter is the worldwide nature of all these things, caves and caverns, pyramids and stones, and strange writings that seem to predate Sanskrit. All these form another piece in our historical puzzle. There are more to come. However, for now, we have established a number of things:

1. Some form of civilization goes far back in time beyond the rise of our own.

2. This civilization has hallmarks of having been worldwide, including evidence in the form of global stone monuments, writing, and strange historical anomalies found around the globe.

3. We have increasing evidence of there having been prior civilizations, such as an actual Atlantis. Several pieces of information would seem to indicate that fabled civilization might actually have been real and precisely where Plato said it was. However, before we discuss this aspect of things in more depth, let's take a close look at the idea of giants.

CHAPTER 6

LAND OF THE GIANTS

Now we come to the land of the giants. This forms yet another big piece of our puzzle. Moreover, it is a necessary one. All around the globe there are legends of these beings. So, we either have to incorporate them into our jigsaw puzzle, or somehow manage to dismiss them as being just such things—just made-up stories and myths. Are there pieces of evidence to support the idea there could have been actual giants? If so, what were they really? Just who were these giants, and how big were they?

Well, according to the stories, they seem to have varied in size. Furthermore, some people insist they are not just legends. For instance, those who believe in the literal word of the Bible do believe in the story of David and the giant, Goliath. The interesting thing about this tale is that it even implies the giant is a rarity in the time of the young King David to be. The Bible also speaks of a race of beings, otherwise known as the Watchers, who were giants in size.

Still, the Bible isn't alone in its stories about giants. This idea also seems true of many legends and myths from around the world. Moreover, one of the common recurring themes of stories about these creatures, no matter where in the world they come from, is that they weren't large in numbers, even if they were large.

They apparently didn't procreate much. Again, this is a common thread through many of the world's tales of giants.

Therefore, the idea giants once existed isn't perhaps quite as crazy as one might think. In fact, tales of giants abound in the ancient cultures of the world. So pervasive are the stories of them around the planet, that even here in America, an entire show on the network A&E (Arts and Entertainment), recently devoted a complete series to the question, with each episode an hour long. The name of the series is, *Search For The Lost Giants.* Episodes of this program are available on YouTube for those readers who might want to watch them.

However, just what are some of the stories of giants? Well, again we can turn to the Bible for one such tale:

"There were giants in the earth in those days; and also after that, when the sons of God came in unto the daughters of men, and they bear children to them, the same became mighty men which were of old, men of renown.—Genesis 6:4."

Based on this, many believe that the hybrid offspring of this mixing of the two races resulted in the long-lived people of the Bible, as well as accounting for some of the mightier kings of ancient times. Do we have any corroborating evidence for this being true? Alternatively, is it just a nice tale from a religious book?

Well, there does seem to be some evidence for long-lived kings from another source. Moreover, this comes from an unlikely source, the *Sumerian List of Kings.* As one researcher put it:

"The list blends prehistorical, presumably mythical predynastic rulers enjoying implausibly lengthy reigns with later, more plausibly historical dynasties."

Notice the emphasis on *"presumably mythical?"* The researcher is hedging his bets here, it seems, and sounds unsure if they really were just mythical or not.

Furthermore, there are cross references to these rulers in other sources, as well. In the *Epic of Gilgamesh*, one of these kings is also mentioned. In fact, some historians argue that Gilgamesh might have been one of these kings, as well. All these antediluvian kings seem to have lived if not impossibly, then improbably long lives by today's standards. They also seem to have been very tall in stature and possessed of certain extra capabilities.

Found on an ancient block of stone, the *List of Kings* was written in ancient Sumerian, cuneiform writing. Since then, more versions of it have been found. So here, we have two Middle Eastern sources for the idea of giants. One was the ancient civilization of Sumeria, forerunners of the Babylonians, and the other was the Old Testament of the Bible. Something else to take note of is the fact that the *Epic of Gilgamesh* shows marked similarities to other cultures' stories of ancient times. These include the legends about the Egyptian God, Osiris. They also are very similar to tales of Hercules, in both the Greek and Roman versions.

Nonetheless, before anyone even thought to begin writing the Bible, legends of giants were already widespread. Passed down from one generation to the next, we have stories of giants also coming from such areas as Greece, Egypt, Rome, China, and many other regions of the world. The parallels of the stories are also amazingly consistent, regardless of where around the world they came from.

Always, somehow, gods or goddesses, have something to do with the creation of the giants. Often, their creation was the result of the intermixing of humans with these gods. In many stories, the giants are a special race, more than mere mortals, but less than the gods. They are often referred to as demigods for this reason, or "smallgods," and the result of a human breeding with a god. But tales from all over do speak of these creatures.

For instance, the blind Greek poet, Homer, said, *"On the earth there once were giants."*

1. **Native Americans.** In North America, many of the Native American tribes also have tales of giants. Tribes, widespread across the continent, as well as those of the Northeast, Canada, and Mexico talk of giants. Some of the stories say these beings existed before the Native Americans arrived, were approximately 3.66 meters in height, and possessed of red hair. They were also considered highly aggressive and dangerous, although they were not in great numbers. Then,

because of their size and abilities, they didn't need to be in large numbers to wreak havoc if they chose, it seems.

Oddly, there seems to be some physical evidence to support these legends of the Native Americans. In the 1920s, several fossil skeletons were found. These included the remains of a male, who had towered over 2.44 meters in height. A female skeleton was over 1.83 meters in height.

Considering how short the Native Americans were, as were most peoples of ancient times, these were truly giants to them. Even today, someone attaining the height of1.83 meters is the extreme rarity. Again, in 1931, a couple more skeletons were found in Nevada. These varied from 2.44 to 3.05 meters in height, and made headlines around the country at the time.

2. **Turkey, 1950s, Giant Skeletons were Claimed to Have Been Unearthed.** In turkey, even more skeletons of giants became known, and again at the time, this caused a big reaction in the news media of the day. Of course, in some cases such things could well be hoaxes. However, in other cases, actual bones and skulls exist, which are definitely not hoaxes.

Nor should we leave out the northern Europeans when it comes to tales of giants. Norse legends of their gods referred to giants, as well. Such beings helped to defeat the gods at the ultimate great conflict of Ragnarok. Besides this, the Norse had legends of a frost giant, as well as of a mountain giant. They also mention a race of giants who fought the gods, the Jotun.

However, giants, as with humans, it seems, were not all of the same type or height. Some seem to have varied in size, being a great deal more than two meters in height in some areas of the world, while others were closer to one and one-half to two meters in height. In other regions, we have tales of truly "giant" giants, who were four, five, and more meters in height. Again, practically every civilization and culture seems to have legends and myths concerning these huge beings. These often seem to have some basis in fact.

3. **"Giant" Native Americans Found In Florida.** On the keys of the Atlantic side of Florida, near what is now Cape Canaveral, a number of skeletons were found in a burial mound. This was during a 1930s archaeological dig. At one burial site, a mass grave of ninety-six skeletons was found. Oddly, the funerary arrangement of the skeletons was in a large circle. The skulls of the skeletons were directed toward the center of the mound with the rest of each skeleton radiating out from that center, rather like spokes.

The age of this race of Native Americans, when they lived, is in some dispute, with some archaeologists saying they were as recent as 3000 years, but others insisting they were far older, dating back as far as 10,000 years ago. The burial mound contains forty-two females, thirty-five males, as well as seven of indeterminate sex, along with twelve child skeletons of various ages. A crystal necklace, a shell, a copper snake, and other artifacts were buried with the skeletons.

The finds show these people were not an isolated group, but must have traded with others, since there is no copper ore in Florida or nearby. Where exactly, the copper came from is a question. Moreover, nobody seems to know who these people were, or where they came from, or for that matter what happened to them. That they were a "robust" people goes without saying. They were very tall. The skulls were unusually thick-boned, and the other bones of the body were huge and very heavy. This has made some researchers refer to them as "giants."

4. **Giant Skull Found in 1940.** Claimed to be possibly the largest skull ever found, on earth, the skull was discovered Victoria County, Texas. Two other skulls also discovered at the same location were not so large, but still very big by normal human standards.

Texas seems to like to claim giants in its ancestry. For instance, in 1900, on September 28, a newspaper reported skeletons of giants found buried near Galveston. They unearthed these just before the hurricane, Isaac, caused such a catastrophe there.

The article claims nearly 2000 giant skeletons were discovered. Researchers claimed they felt this was a result of a tidal wave, which had wiped out this prehistoric settlement. The researchers claim there are also two levels of the skeletons, thus indicating two separate inundations by tidal waves (tsunamis?).

The discovery was the result of explorers attempting to find artifacts for an exhibit on archaeology. The article goes on to say the skulls were undoubtedly at least several thousand years old, and probably more. A Mr. Simmons, the superintendent of the Arizona and New Mexico railway was overseeing excavations along the line in Galveston County. It was then the bones became known.

The article claims that, along with the skeletons, pieces of ivory and various artifacts had been buried. The number of skeletons discovered would seem to indicate these were a large community of people.

The article also states that several thousand skeletons were removed, with some 1500 discovered in the first excavation. An oddity is that no bones of children seemed to have been discovered. Either that or the skeletons were so large the discoverers simply didn't recognize them as children, perhaps. The two sets of skeletons were in two distinct layers of strata.

5. **Giant Stone Hammers and Other Tools Discovered in North and South America.** As just two examples of this phenomenon of finding oversized implements in the Americas, we have a giant ax discovered in Manitoba, Canada. This discovery was by Murray Hiebert, an archaeologist. The ax is real. Photographs of it are available. Either a very, very large person wielded this ax, or it had some ornamental purpose. Exactly, what kind is impossible to say. If so, a great deal of effort has gone into the making of such an "ornament." Another oversized hammer, this one made of stone, was found in Ecuador. Moreover, the hammer was far too big for the average human to try to wield.

6. **Meter-High Giants?** Speaking of Ecuador, several people found skeletons exposed on a crumbling mountain. Measurements

of the fragments showed the skeletons were huge in size. For example, a heel bone measured five times the size of an average human's. A section of the occipital region of the skull was approximately five times that of a human. This would mean the person who had this skeleton stood as much as some ten meters tall!

7. **Giant Mummy Index Finger in 1988.** In 1988, a grave robber in Egypt claimed he had come across a very large "blond" mummy. Apparently, this was sometime in the 1960s, originally. Later, in 2012, photographs of the giant mummified finger were published in a German newspaper, The *Bild-Zeitung*. The finger is some 38.1 centimeters long, as compared to the average index finger of humans today, which is only about 10.16 centimeters in length. By extrapolation, this would mean the person who originally had this finger would have been about 6.1 meters tall! X-rays done on the finger indicate it is not that of an animal. So just who did this giant finger belong to?

8. **Giant Skull in Barcelona Museum.** Here, we have another case of an oversized object with regard to human remains. A Spanish researcher and writer by the name of Joseph Guijarro claimed the discovery of an oversized human skull. This was found in a long unused storage area of the Archaeological Museum of Barcelona. It was as if it was hidden there.

No explanation for the skull has been forthcoming, and it seems archaeologists have largely simply chosen to ignore it. However the skull is real and it is a giant skull by modern-day, human measurements. Nobody seems to be able to account for the thing. Even its origin seems to be a mystery. Moreover, nobody can or will explain why the skull was hidden for so long, except that perhaps, the Catholic Church at one time held a lot of power in Spain, and for this reason, it was thought best to hide something that might be seen as heretical, perhaps.

9. A Blond-Haired Mummy in China. On May 14, 2015, the China daily newspaper reported the discovery of a blonde-haired mummy. Location of the find was in Xinjiang. There, in the dunes of the sparsely settled region, Liao Zhaoyu, along with several colleagues, found a large coffin. The coffin was made of wood, was "boat-shaped," and was very long. Liao Zhaoyu made a joke of it by saying he thought they might have found the casket of a giant. Giants had long been a part of the myths about ancient China, and so were and are an integral part of Chinese folklore.

When they opened the coffin, they saw a blonde-haired mummy. He was approximately two and a quarter meters in length. The mummy, when alive, would have been even taller than that, and would have topped out at over 2.44 meters tall. A great deal of excitement resulted from this discovery of a member of a "tribe of giants." Nor was this the only such coffin found there. As a result, locals refer to the region, one composed mostly of drifting sand dunes, as "the Valley of the Giants."

The strange part is the mummy has rather European features, or rather those of some ancient Europeans. With blond hair, relatively high cheekbones, and of course, being much taller than the current inhabitants of the region, the mummy appears distinctly out of place for the area. The newspaper also reported the burial area is a vast one. Farmers in the 1980s had attempted to rework sand dunes to be able to grow crops there. In the process, they came across other coffins. Sadly, they used much of the wood to make fires, and so did much damage to the site in the process.

In 2013, scientists in Belfast, Northern Ireland, at the Queen's University, after careful analysis, declared the remains probably dated back to at least 4600 years ago. The researchers determined the coffins were of the desert poplar. These trees still grow in the area. Despite damage from the farmers and tomb raiders, five complete mummies have been found at the locale.

Other mummies were not far away. These included one of a woman, who later received the nickname, "The Beauty of Xiaohe."

She, along with thirty other mummies, had been buried about the area. Again, they date back to roughly 4000 or more years ago.

This find, along with all the others, has huge implications. The elaborate burial methods, the incredible size of these people, being over 2.44 meters tall, along with the various artifacts found, suggests a large and well-developed civilization once existed in the region. Nor was this civilization populated by the ancestors of the inhabitants who live there today. These are people unknown. Although European in appearance, their height is not in the least normal, certainly not by European standards now or then.

10. **Giant Remains in Bulgaria.** In the City of Varna, the remains of a "huge skeleton" were unearthed. Varna, situated on the edge of the Black Sea, has a long history, with archaeological finds dating back to more than 7000 years ago, and some say even longer.

The skeleton would appear to be male and the age is believed to date back to somewhere around 500 to 400 BCE. The area in which the archaeologists discovered the skeleton was the location of Odessos, a Greek colony established there around 700 BCE.

One archaeologist, Valeria Yotov has stated the bones belong to "a very tall man," but did not say just how tall. The implication was the skeleton was strikingly tall and so most unusual in its height. The use of the word "giant" is often used to describe the remains.

11. **Giant Warrior Skeleton Found in Romania.** In 2013, an even older skeleton was found in Romania, near Santa Mare. The skeleton, that of a warrior, is well over two meters tall. Subsequently, and based on this fact, the skeleton received the nickname of Goliath. What makes this find all the more impressive was the average height of a person was far less in that region at the time, being only one-and-a-half meters in height at most. This skeleton, based on preliminary findings, is said to date to around 1600 BCE.

12. Giant Skeletons Found In Wisconsin. This is a peculiar story, one of many such that appeared in newspapers all over the United States on and off from the mid 1850s up to and around the early 1900s. This one deals with giant skeletons reported found close by Lake Delavan, Wisconsin, in May of 1912. This was an actual archaeological dig-site, one primarily conducted by the Beloit College at the time. The researchers were investigating no less than 200 mounds. However, what they unearthed at one point took them by complete surprise.

Skeletons were exhumed, eighteen of them, and they were huge. The skeletal remains ranged in height from a minimum of around 2.29 meters. Furthermore, they had outsized skulls, even for such large skeletons. Additionally, the skulls were elongated, as has been reported from excavations in other places around the world. The discoverers claimed the skulls had two rows of teeth, and a number of the skeletons had six toes and six fingers.

The newspaper article of the time openly wondered if these were not giants of the Bible, and the article even referred to Genesis 6:4. Likewise, this is not an isolated case. By the time this article had gone to press, over 200 other such discoveries of giant remains already had been unearthed around the country. It was only in the mid-twentieth century that most newspapers stopped reporting such discoveries, although a number of such were still made. It is assumed that mainstream science had quelled the idea of giants, so much so that such discoveries had to be hoaxes in their opinion, and thus went largely unreported.

In addition, it should be noted finds of giant skeletons weren't the rule among the ancient Mound Builder sites, but rather the exception. Again, the "giants" seemed to be scarce in numbers compared to their more normal human counterparts. It should also be noted that the six fingers and six toes are not quite the oddity they seem. Humans often are born with just the same sort of thing, including webbing between fingers and toes. Anne Boleyn, second wife of Henry XIII, is said to have had six fingers, for example.

Does this mean we are somehow related to these giants in some fashion, share some common DNA? It is possible, since there is no evidence to suppose the two races couldn't intermingle to reproduce. However, there are legends of normal human women having died in trying to give birth to such possible hybrid offspring, and these, too, come from around the world.

So in conclusion of this chapter, what do we make of this idea giants ones strode the surface of our Earth? Well, there does seem to be actual evidence for the idea. Discoveries of bones and skulls seem to show their habitat to have been worldwide. Although their height varied, other factors about them did not. Again, according to all the written records, as well as oral traditions, they were long-lived, but few in numbers. They were formidable when it came to fighting, and humans were afraid of them, and for good reason, it seems. Apparently, the very earliest days of our current civilization, some giants seem to have still existed, perhaps as with Goliath of David and Goliath. By this time, they were very few in numbers and virtually an extinct race, it would appear.

Nevertheless, if one goes by the recorded evidence of such stories as the *Epic of Gilgamesh*, Genesis in the Bible, and other tales of these creatures, there were greater numbers of these "giants" a long time ago. It is important to note, as well, that legends often speak of great battles involving giants. Again, the fall of the Norse gods is one example. There are more.

As one major instance of this, we have the "Nephilim." Supposedly existing before the Great Flood, the word refers to ancient inhabitants of the region of Canaan, and around the time, the Israelites decided to make it their home. Thus, we again have that reference to David fighting Goliath. Still earlier on in history, according to the Bible, there were more. The Nephilim, as mentioned earlier, were supposedly the "sons of God" (some translators read this as, "sons of gods"), who it is said intermarried with humans, thus producing this race of hybrids, part human, and part something else (apparently, according to some Biblical/Hebrew texts, "angels" did the interbreeding).

This offshoot race became the ancient and powerful rulers of the region prior to the Great Flood. They were possessed of very long lives, according to the List of Kings.

The Bible, if one can take it as being at all reliable as a record of history, speaks of equally long-lived people, as well, such as Methuselah, Noah, Adam, and others. Furthermore, these people were supposed to be possessed of great strength, often great size, and other abilities, such as high intellects, as well. The ancient Sumerians also refer to something very similar when they described their history of the Anunnaki. So the hybrid offspring were exceptional beings, by all accounts.

Yes, many have heard of these people before, of course, but we mention them here for several reasons:

1. Many stories of the Great Flood center around the idea that one of the reasons, if not the main reason for the flood, was God's way of exterminating the Nephilim, whom he considered unworthy, and a bad influence on humans.

2. They were teaching us things God supposedly didn't want humans to know. The titan god, Prometheus of Greek mythology, for example, was severely punished for teaching humans about fire, and was ordered to be tortured for eternity as his fate for daring to do such a thing.

3. Whatever one calls them, the Nephilim or giants, they are important, because they keep popping up in various legends and myths in one form or another around the world. The Nephilim, by the way, were also referred to as "Watchers," although who or what they were watching is a bit vague. Most think they were watching us humans. Some of the more religious think this was for God, at his directive, and others think it was for someone else, a race of extraterrestrials, for example.

Others have argued that since modern humans and Neanderthals existed for a period of several thousand years together, and according to modern scientists were able to interbreed with us, that perhaps these "giants" were a hybrid race of Neanderthals and ourselves. The problem with this idea is, Neanderthals died out long before the period in which the Israelites invaded Canaan, by thousands of years. If some few had managed to survive and interbreed, there is also the problem of their height. In general, Neanderthals were shorter than we were, so a hybrid race would not likely be taller.

Can we say for sure giants existed? Well, some very tall people seem to have. In addition, these tall people (*very* tall in some cases) seem to have existed in places around the globe. If not giants, then who and what were they? That they were not the "norm" is obvious. So what happened to the giants? Where did they go? If humans had a hard time beating them in battle, what did bring about their downfall? This is another puzzle piece of our timeline and we will deal with it later on in more depth.

CHAPTER 7

WORLDWIDE PYRAMIDS

We are well aware of the fact of pyramids being scattered all about the place in Egypt, as well as Central America. What may not be generally known is more pyramids have been discovered in Egypt in recent times, in large part, thanks to satellite imagery. Seemingly, there are quite a number of them, buried, according to the same satellite images. These have been buried over time, and so were lost to history. Yet, they are there, and they are significant.

This is major news for the world of archaeology. Up until recently, it was thought that pyramids in Egypt were rather rare. After all, they were reserved for pharaohs. This, they may still have been, but there are more pyramids spotted about Egypt than was initially thought and not necessarily in centralized locations. Either some of the pharaoh-kings were having themselves interred at various locales scattered throughout the kingdom, or something else was going on, some other reason for the construction of such massive edifices. Just what that "something" might be is still unknown.

Furthermore, what many of the public may not know is the extent of pyramid building with regard to other regions of the world, as well. Pyramids, it seems, are a truly global phenomenon. They were hardly restricted to Egypt or the New World. Nobody seems to know why this is so, this great spate of global pyramid building that once was so popular. However, it is a fact, and we still have many of those pyramids today.

For instance, China seems to have quite a few pyramids and in various sizes. What's more, until recently we knew very little about them. The Chinese Communist government has long been a secretive one. Only recently, with the opening up of its markets to the world, and as more information begun to flow, did the rest of the planet become aware of these pyramids.

Moreover, pyramids come in several basic varieties, it seems. Either they are like the pyramids of Giza, rising to a relatively sharp point, or they are of the step variety, as in the Yucatan Peninsula. Some have a flattened top. Then there are those of the mound variety, of having been built more as earthen works than stone pyramids.

Yet, these are definitely pyramidal in shape, as well. Only the method and means to build them is different. China is a good example of this. Near the city of Xi'an are a number of pyramids. These are of the mound type, as mentioned above. They lie in fields, scattered about in various clusters. These are a relatively new discovery, only having been found in the latter half of the twentieth century.

As with most pyramids built out of mounds, these tend to have a flattened top to them, much as the stone pyramids throughout the Yucatan Peninsula and elsewhere in Central and North America seem to have been. The pyramids in the Chinese fields come in various sizes and heights, and can be as high as sixty-one meters, and as low as 6.1. They can vary in width from a top limit of 183 meters down to just 15.24.

The age of some of them is not in dispute, with perhaps the oldest one being about 2500 years old. However, there are several pyramids just north of Beijing, as well as in Inner Mongolia. Some of these are very old and predate the beginning of modern civilization by about 2000 years. The dates on them vary, but they are between 4700 and 2900 BCE.

1. **Pyramids In The New World.** We must also mention the fact of the huge pyramids found in and near the Yucatan Peninsula. These rival the Pyramids of Giza in size, and in some ways, are even more impressive. They are step pyramids for the most part, and many have yet to even be excavated.

2. **Gunung Padang.** This was a surprise to archaeologists worldwide. Thought to have been just a hill with steps shaped into it, Gunung Padang turned out to be a step pyramid, instead. Again, we have the controversy over the age of the structure. First thought to date back somewhere in the range of 500 to 1500 BCE, based on radiocarbon dating of structures on the surface, this was later brought into question. It seems these structures might have been built at a later date, much later than the pyramid itself, since core samples of the basalt carved structures, which went deep below the surface, showed very different results. Some of the columns, the material surrounding them at around 27.43 meters below the surface, were radiocarbon dated from 22,000 to 20,000 BCE, making them 22,000 to 24,000 years old!

3. **Pyramids in the Canary Islands.** Near Guimar on Tenerife, there are flat-topped pyramids. The famous Thor Heyerdahl brought them to everyone's attention when he investigated them back in 1980. These pyramids are composed of blocks of stone.

4. **Pyramids in Mauritius.** Mauritius, an island off the eastern African coast, has seven pyramids. These pyramids, for all practical purposes, seem to be the same as those found on the Island of Tenerife, which is far away, indeed, being on the opposite side of the continent of Africa. It should be noted the pyramids were built ages before there was any Suez Canal to shorten a trip from the Mediterranean to Mauritius, so whoever built these was either:

a. Local to the area, which seems unlikely, since the pyramids are virtually identical to the ones in Tenerife, or

b. The same culture/civilization built both sets of pyramids, despite the vast distances between them.

However, just who these pyramid builders might have been is a mystery. Mauritius has been known for a long time. Arabs knew of it as far back as the tenth century, CE, although it wasn't until over 500 years later the Italians actually added it in their maps.

So who built the pyramids? Well, here we get into the land of "surmise" as archaeologists seem to have no real idea, but only guesses. The "surmise" in this case is the pyramids on both Tenerife and Mauritius might have been built by the ancestors of the Sea Peoples. These were a group of people who existed in the Mediterranean prior to the advent of even the Phoenicians.

Alternatively, it might have been the Phoenicians, themselves, who discovered the island, but we have no way of knowing for sure, since nothing of either culture has been found on Mauritius. The Sea Peoples, if they did this, must have accomplished the task well before 600 BCE, or possibly even further back in time. One Phoenician expedition supposedly circumnavigated Africa, but whether these people discovered the island and then later inhabited it, is strictly a matter for conjecture.

To date, there is simply no evidence to show this. However, again, there are seven pyramids on Mauritius, and like those of Tenerife, they do not go above twelve meters in height. They have a maximum of eleven steps making them up, and they seem to be constructed of a different sort of limestone. On some of the pyramids, a layer of basalt covers the limestone blocks. As to whether all of the pyramids were originally designed this way, with such a basalt outer cover, is uncertain. Some of the pyramids have been tampered with, apparently to use some of the materials making them up, so one simply can't be sure. Since the pyramids are made of stone, dating them, as well, is very difficult and no reliable age has yet been assigned to them.

5. **Monk Mound Pyramid, United States.** Built by a people that inhabited the Midwest area, the so-called Mound Builders, there is an earthen pyramid located close by the Mississippi River, near East St. Louis, Illinois, just a few kilometers from the Mississippi River. Called "Cahokia," this civilization had some truly large earthen pyramids. And Cahokia was the largest of the Mesoamerican cultures in the United States. Theoretically, the Cahokia did not have writing, and their civilization flourished around 1200 CE, having at its peak a population of approximately 40,000. This may not seem large, but at the time, this metropolis had a greater population than that of London, England, of the same period. Then, abruptly, it seems the civilization simply ended. The reason for this is not known.

6. **The Rest of the World.** Pyramids and pyramidal structures have been found in many other places around the world, as well. These include locations in Spain, Italy, Great Britain, Germany, Turkey, France, and even Greece, as well as possibly in Romania. Whether constructed of earth, stones, or a combination, pyramids seem to be a worldwide phenomenon that date far back in time for the most part.

7. **Pyramids in Antarctica?** In a more recent development, in 2002, claims that the buried ruins of an ancient city in Antarctica were found spread like wildfire over the Internet. What's more, there were also claims of three "Giza-style pyramids" having been discovered, one near the coast, and two a little further inland. Photographs of the pyramids, mostly covered in ice and snow, do definitely look like the great Pyramids of Giza in shape and relative size. However, just going by the photographs, it is impossible to say if these are very good natural ones, or artificial in nature without closer examination.

With regard to the ruins, Jonathan Gray, an archaeologist, has made these claims. He also says the United States government is trying to stop the airing of a video made by a news team with regard to the find. The ruins are said to be buried under no less than 3200 meters of ice, so bringing the ancient city to light would be an arduous task. Furthermore, the report says that despite this fact, a dig is "already underway" there, apparently a government sponsored one.

A spokesman for the company is reported to have said at the time that:

"The US government said it will seek to block the airing of a video found by navy rescuers in Antarctica that purportedly reveals that a massive archaeological dig is underway two miles (3200 meters) beneath the ice."

8. **How Many Pyramids Are There In Total?** Something else to consider is the sheer number of pyramids. For example, going by relatively recent infrared satellite photographs, a mainstream archaeologist, Dr Sarah Parcak of the University of Alabama, has discovered what appear to be no less than seventeen more pyramids buried beneath the earth's surface in Egypt.

Besides this, there are what appear to be more than,1000 tombs, as well, and this isn't even counting the number of ancient settlements. This is in Egypt alone. So the idea of knowing how many pyramids there are around the world is a figure that is not only fluid, but subject to change and often. One thing we do know; there are a lot of them, and that number keeps growing.

9. **An Oddity.** With regard to the main pyramids, the larger ones, these seem to fall within a very narrow line around the world. They are all situated close to the same latitude. Many investigators have discussed and debated if there is a possible reason why this might have been done deliberately, or whether it is just a fluke. To date, nobody has a definitive answer on this.

Also, as we have shown here, the Constellation of Orion seems to figure prominently in some way or other with pyramids. Whether with the small Eye of the Pyramid in Ecuador, or the giant pyramids of Giza, we have a connection to Orion. There has been a lot of conjecture as to why this is, but no one seems to know for sure. The fact that it is worldwide in nature also is a curious thing, indeed. Not only is the construction of pyramids a global phenomenon, but it seems their connection to Orion is, as well.

So, how do we account for this seeming global love affair with pyramids? Did various cultures and civilizations worldwide just chance on the same idea...over and over again? This would seem unlikely. Do humans have some intrinsic urge to build pyramids, more so than other forms of structures? Again, this would seem unlikely, as well.

So how do we account for this global obsession with building pyramids? Perhaps, and this would seem the simplest explanation, a global culture/civilization had not only the knowledge of how to build them, had some reason for building them, but also disseminated that knowledge around the planet. This would be an easy thing to do, if there was a global civilization with means and methods of communication worldwide. Again, this would seem the most likely answer. Judging by the age of some of the pyramids, this culture could have dated as far back as 12,000 years ago, and some say much more.

As with the stone monuments around the world, the age of pyramid building came to a sudden end, although it seems at different times in different places. All around the world, with only minor exceptions, this seems to have been the case. Moreover, later stone monument constructions, and most later-period pyramids do not match their forerunners in size and complexity, or numbers. It is almost as if they were built at the close of another time, another age, and by the remnants of a dying civilization, one that could no longer attain the architectural heights of their own forebears.

Alternatively, it is possible that another people built the later ones, and were mimicking the mightier ones of those who had come before them. We simply can't be sure at this point. Still, today, no stone pyramids of the types once built are being created, or have been recently been created. The Age of Pyramids seems definitely over.

However, we do have other examples of this sort of thing. Stone monuments of the Stagnant Period of human history; the later ones are of a lesser variety, usually having much smaller stones than those of 12,000 years ago, with few exceptions. The more recent the stone monuments, the less impressive they tend to be. It's almost as if people were trying to duplicate the efforts of others who came before them, but just weren't managing the same level of abilities.

Even in Egypt we see this. The greatest constructions, the most impressive pyramids were built early on in that civilization's history. Then, for some reason, pyramid building just came to a halt. For later pharaohs and their people, the Pyramids of Giza were already of great antiquity, their origins lost in myth. Moreover, nobody attempted to build on such a scale every again in that civilization. In other words, Egypt was at its peak in this ability early on. As time passed, its capabilities became less in this regard, rather than more, as one would logically think would happen, as they would have amassed more knowledge of such things over time. But no, the reverse is true. As time passed, they seemed to lose their ability to create such marvelous edifices. This is directly opposite of what has been happening with our present civilization. As time passes, we learn more and so are able to build even better structures.

CHAPTER 8

SUNKEN CITIES

I'm sure all those with an interest in these topics have heard and perhaps even read much, and seen more on the subject of lost civilizations. Notably, the one always mentioned is Atlantis. Rightfully so, perhaps, because this civilization now lost to us, seems to strike a chord within us.

However, there are other lost civilizations, as well. Many people have heard of these, too. I'm talking about Lemuria and Mu. But what people often don't realize is there is evidence for more such lost civilizations. Actually, many more.

In fact, cultures and civilizations around the world all have their myths and legends of lost or sunken cities. Some have real evidence to support the idea. However, let's start with the most famous and obvious of them all:

1. **Atlantis.** This is such a well-known story, that I won't dwell on it long here. However, I would like to point out that in many cases, recent researchers have gone further and further afield in their attempts to locate and prove the existence of Atlantis. Although, I applaud their efforts, I think they are largely unnecessary. It is probably best just to stick with the simple facts, as we already know them.

The legend of Atlantis comes down to us directly from Plato. Therefore, as far as I'm concerned, since he's the original and final word on the subject of Atlantis, we simply need to go by what he said. If Atlantis existed, then Plato was the first to speak of it and so it is his voice we should listen to about this.

So who was Plato? Well, he was a noted philosopher who lived in the final years of the Golden Age of Pericles, when the city-state of Athens was at its zenith. This places the time of Plato about 2400 years before our time, approximately.

Sadly, Plato only briefly described his Atlantis for us. He didn't give us very much to go on. Nonetheless, he did say the legendary place existed about 9000 years before his time, or about 11,400 years before ours. He also said the island lay "beyond the Pillars of Hercules," and so was situated in the Atlantic. He described the city in some detail, being one with concentric canals circling the center of the city, which in turn, lay in the center of a plain. This means that Atlantis, its greatest city, lay at a low level, probably not far above sea level, if canals had been necessary to drain what easily could have been marshland. Here is Plato's own description of Atlantis, its location, and history:

"For it is related in our records how once upon a time your State stayed the course of a mighty host, which, starting from a distant point in the Atlantic ocean, was insolently advancing to attack the whole of Europe, and Asia to boot. For the ocean there was at that time navigable; for in front of the mouth which you Greeks call, as you say, 'the pillars of Heracles,' there lay an island which was larger than Libya and Asia together; and it was possible for the travelers of that time to cross from it to the other islands, and from the islands to the whole of the continent over against them which encompasses that veritable ocean. For all that we have here, lying within the mouth of which we speak, is evidently a haven having a narrow entrance; but that yonder is a real ocean, and the land surrounding it may most rightly be called, in the fullest and truest sense, a continent. Now in this island of Atlantis there existed a confederation of kings, of great

and marvelous power, which held sway over all the island, and over many other islands also and parts of the continent."
—From Plato's *Dialogue of Timaeus*, 360 BCE.

Many researchers/archaeologists don't think Atlantis was in the Atlantic Ocean. Instead, they believe the story of Atlantis was derived from the actual historical event of the explosion of the caldera volcano, Thera. This volcano was on the island of current-day Santorini, off the coast of Greece in the southern Aegean Sea.

Archaeologists and radiocarbon experts are in some disagreement as to the exact date of the eruption that destroyed the Minoan civilization of the times. Archaeologists say, according to their evidence, the eruption occurred around 1500 BCE. Radiocarbon dating experts push the event back further in time to 1600 or 1650 BCE. However, this is only a 100-to-150 year discrepancy, at most.

In any case, this puts the eruption (if we go by the archaeologists' stated time of the event) at just about 900 to 1000 years before the time of Plato. Those who argue the destruction of the Minoan civilization is what Plato was really talking about when he mentioned Atlantis, point to the fact that Plato said 9000 years before his time. Drop one zero from that and one has 900 years, instead. They say the 9000 years was just a mistake and that Plato meant 900 years before his time.

However, as intriguing as it might be to think the Thera eruption was what Plato was referring to, it ignores several glaring facts. Plato specifically states Atlantis was beyond the Pillars of Hercules. Some archaeologists argue he didn't mean the Strait of Gibraltar, that there were narrow straits far closer to Greece also named the same thing. This is very unlikely. The Greeks were a seafaring people and had been for several centuries, at least, by the time of Plato. They had planted colonies all over the coastlines of the Mediterranean, including in France, Italy, the Island of Sicily, along the coastlines of the Black Sea, the Adriatic, as well as along the coastal regions of North Africa. The Greek civilization, including not only Athens, but also many other maritime city states, planted about 500 such colonies by the start of the Age of Pericles in Athens, around 500 BCE.

Again, Plato was born in the last part of this Golden Age of Athens, and so was fully aware of the geography of the times. He undoubtedly knew, being born and raised to the nobility, as well as being well educated, just where the Pillars of Hercules were, as well as the Atlantic Ocean. Moreover, he refers directly to the "real ocean," which he pointedly references as not being part of the Mediterranean. Therefore, it is unlikely Plato was referring to the volcanic eruption of Thera only some 900 years before his time. This means he did not mean the Minoan Civilization when he spoke of Atlantis. Atlantis, according to Plato, clearly lay in the Atlantic Ocean and did have nearby smaller islands (Canary Islands?).

Is there any evidence to support the contention there actually was an Atlantis at this location? After all, so many locations have been suggested as the "true location" of Atlantis, the issue is rather blurred. Well, there is one intriguing bit of evidence, hard evidence that would seem to suggest Plato was being accurate about the location of his "lost island." That evidence is the World Stone Map.

2. **World Stone Map and Atlantis.** Mentioned earlier, but now here in more detail, the World Stone Map is a most interesting artifact, and constitutes another one of those "oopart" anomalies. Discovered in 1984, in Ecuador, the World Stone Map is a definite oddity. Not large, and having a natural ovoid shape, it also has a natural line of white mineral running through it about where an equator would be on the globe of Earth. The stone also has engravings of what can only be a world map. The map clearly depicts North and South America, as well as Europe, Asia, and Africa. There also are references to Greenland and Iceland, as well.

On the area depicting the Middle East, somewhere near Jerusalem, is an inlaid stone "eye." This is quite definitely an eye in appearance and shape. The meaning of this eye can only seem to have something to do with its location. In addition, the features on the east coast of Asia show an elongated peninsula, both larger and much longer than the Indonesian Peninsula of today. This helps to date the stone to around 10,000 to 12,000 BCE, or even much earlier, since the world sea level was much lower at the time and so there was more land. This would be in keeping with how the landmasses are depicted on the stone, being more extensive and connected.

However, there is one more thing. The Word Stone Map clearly shows a large island in the Atlantic Ocean. This is exactly the location Plato described for his Atlantis. Modern maps, of course, do not show this land mass, because it isn't there. Yet, on the World Stone Map, which is accurate in every other respect, it is. The Map of the World was discovered not far from a place known as having the "best water in the world." This water contains silver and gold in it, in a colloidal suspension. It is named "Aqua Vite," or in English, Water of Life, and many wonder if this wasn't the source for the legend of the "Fountain of Youth."

We do have some questions about the World Stone Map. How could "they," whoever "they" were, make a world map that depicts our planet, as it was over 12,000 years ago? Why did they put the "eye" inlay so near current day Jerusalem and the Temple of the Mount? Archaeologists have little doubt (according to them) that Jerusalem did not exist so long ago, so why place the eye there if nothing was there? Or was there? Had the Temple of the Mount platform already been built?

Furthermore, off the island of Bimini, what are now identified as "artifacts," were found anchors made of stone, as well as the now-famous "Bimini Road." With regard to this last, there is still an ongoing and strong debate over whether this feature is natural or not. Those claiming it is artificial in nature, point to the carved stone anchors found in the immediate area as further proof they are right. Still, some ancient civilization was using stone anchors there, not far from where the World Stone Map shows a very large island once may have existed.

3. **The Eye of the Sahara.** This is something that has to be mentioned, as well, because of its similarity in design to Plato's description Atlantis, and the fact it is a very large and strange planetary anomaly. The Eye of the Sahara, or as it is more properly known, the Richat Structure is so large it can clearly be seen from space. In addition, from space, it looks for all the world like a large blue eye staring up from the Sahara Desert in Northern Africa.

The strange thing about the Eye of the Sahara, although it is clearly a major geological structure, nobody is sure of exactly how it was formed. The eye is composed of a series of concentric rings (as the capital of Atlantis had). These rings are eroding circles of mountains, or hills. Geologists say the softer stone in between the harder layers erodes faster, thus creating the ring effect of each circle of stone making up the eye. Approximately fifty kilometers in diameter, the Eye is located near the region of Mauritania.

Various theories over time have been advanced to explain this strange geological anomaly. Originally thought to have been volcanic in nature, this has been ruled out. The theory it was the result of a massive meteorite impact, rather like Meteor Crater in Arizona, only larger, has also since been ruled out, for there is no shocked quartz (a sure sign of an asteroid impact) or any other such materials there.

The latest theory is the Eye is an eroded dome of volcanic material. However, the extremely circular nature of it, and the alternating layers of hard and softer stone are hard to account for. Sedimentary rock, that which is laid down on seabed, can have alternating layers of hardness and softness, depending on the material of which they are composed, but for an igneous dome to do this, and be so circular, as well, is not something for which geologists can yet account.

The reason the Eye of the Sahara is included here is because:

a. The eye does closely resemble, geologically, the description of the main city of Atlantis in layout, and

b. The Eye was formed long enough ago there would have been plenty of water in the area. This could allow for some of the circles having been filled with water, as in circular canals. As Plato said:

"There were two of land and three of water [circular rings]..."

Plate also described a mountain of sorts just to the north of the city. In addition, it should be mentioned that "Atlantis" literally meant "Island of Atlas." A mountain range just to the north of the Eye of the Sahara is the actual Atlas range—a very curious coincidence, at the least. Something else: the Sahara once held a huge lake and wetlands area. Pictographs found on rocks in the Sahara Desert show hunters chasing all manner of animals through grasslands there.

Sandy Island. For those who think an island can't disappear without a trace, think again! Sandy Island, in the South Coral Sea. This island has been on charts for several centuries, and now it seems to have just simply vanished. The island, approximately 24.14 kilometers long and 4.83 kilometers wide disappeared recently.

Scientists, and many debunkers, recently claimed the "Mystery of Sandy Island Solved," by saying it never existed in the first place, was just a mistake on an original map, which was then copied.

There are major problems with this idea. First, if the island never existed, why did it show up on a Google Satellite Earth map, but pixelated? Google only does pixilation for government sensitive sites, (such as military bases, etc.) Nevertheless, the island is definitely in the image for all to see.

Secondly, debunkers of the island argued the original discoverers did not discover an island, per se, but an area where there was rough wave action, and breaking waves, so what they thought was an island was really a reef or shoals of a sort.

This, too, is incorrect. Scientists have sailed directly over where the island is supposed to have been, and the water there is deep, very deep! In other words, there never could have been shoals or reefs of any sort there. Furthermore, more than one group spied the island. As one source put it, it was "repeatedly discovered." Therefore, although controversy still rages, given A Google Satellite shows a pixelated version of the island, even showing its shape, something very strange seems to be going on here.

What does this mean? Well, it seems islands can and do disappear, ever after having been "repeatedly discovered" and photographed from space. Whatever happened to Sandy Island, it is a very weird story, at the very least.

However, Atlantis is hardly the only legend of a sunken city. Again, like the legends of giants, these stories abound in different civilizations and cultures around the planet. In Western Europe, in France, there is an intriguing tale. This is the legend of the lost City of Ys. As mentioned in a prior book, *Ancient Alien Empire Megalithia*, many researchers feel that "Ys" or "Is" (the alternate spelling), might have been Atlantis by a different name.

4. **City Of Ys.** Legends claim the City of Ys was a political powerhouse. They also say it was a beautiful city, quite splendid. Said to have been in the Bay of Douarnenez, the city was a place of trade and commerce. It was a center for shipping. Oddly, Cornwall in England (south-westernmost tip of Great Britain) also has the legend, although they named the city as being Lyonesse, the home of the legendary "Tristan" of *Tristan and Iseult* fame (later made into an opera by Wagner). In fact, Lyonesse might be a different city, but so close to the location of Ys is it, according to all available stories, one is inclined to think they are probably the same city. So although Ys lies just west of the coast of France, it was south of Cornwall. This actually gives us a sort of triangulation as to the location of the supposed drowned metropolis.

It should be mentioned that even today, one can see the traces of ancient (Roman?) roads leading down to the water's edge and apparently right on into the sea. This is in the Western region of Brittany, a province of France. The City of Ys would have been just off the coast of that province, if it actually existed and many think it did.

Need more evidence? There is another city that incorporated the name of Ys. Today, it is the capital of France and is the city of Paris. Paris, in an old Breton dialect, means "like Ys" or "like Is." Apparently, so beautiful was the city, the later city of Paris was named in honor of it. There are many legends about Ys. One of them is that during great storms, one can hear the tolling of the submerged bells of the lost city's cathedral. However, it is more likely the city was lost in the sea long before the time Catholicism and cathedrals were introduced to this region of Europe, but again, one can't be sure.

Legends of sunken cities abound and are global. Whether Cornwall, the middle of the Atlantic, the Mediterranean, off the coast of India/Pakistan, Japan, or Indonesia, as well as the Polynesian Pacific area, legends of sunken cities and temples seem to be everywhere.

Are sunken cities a possibility, or are they just fanciful tales? Well, we know there are real sunken cities. For example, there is the recently discovered sunken portion of Alexandria, Egypt. Sections of Cleopatra's palace, as well as other structures, have been found beneath the waters of the Mediterranean. This is a fact. There are more. In the Mulifanua Bay of the Samoan islands, explorers have discovered the ruins and pottery shards of a Lapita village under the sea. The pottery shards date back as far as 800 BCE. At one time, this village had been above water, obviously.

5. **Pavlopetri, Greece.** Off the coast of Laconia is a city that dates back at least 5000 years and quite possibly more. The city is Pavlopetri. It is unique in having a town plan, including streets, buildings, and tombs. Nicholas Fleming discovered the site in 1967. Recent mappings of the sunken city, which is submerged four meters deep, at the shallowest places, covers over 9000 meters in area. Archaeologists think the metropolis may have sunk beneath the waves due to a series of earthquakes around 1000 BCE. Nevertheless, at this point, this is merely conjecture. No one is sure of when the city went beneath the waves. The age of the city is still in question, as

well as many archaeologists believing it dates back at least as far if not farther than 2800 BCE.

6. **Pheia.** There are yet more Grecian sunken cities. Many stories and legends about the ancient Peloponnesian War surrounded the city called Pheia. In 1911, the city was found by explorers some five meters below the sea surface, off the west coast of Greece. The Peloponnesian War took place in the fifth century BCE. Although some research has been done with regard to the sunken city, little real knowledge has yet been achieved, other than the fact of its existence. It is thought earthquakes may have sunk the city at some point not long after that ancient war took place.

7. **Dwarka.** Off the west coast of India, there is another mysterious sunken city, Dwarka. This is a recent discovery, having been found in 2002. Of course, being underwater some 36.57 meters hasn't helped archaeologists to determine a great deal about the city, because of the logistical problems of diving involved. Nevertheless, a true city, it seems to be. It covers an area of approximately25.9 square kilometers. Here is the interesting part; pottery shards show the city dates back at least 9500 years, or possibly quite a bit older, because these are only the shards lying on the surface of the sea floor. It is presumed older pottery shards lay buried there farther down in the sediments. The age is based on carbon dating.

Moreover, this sunken city of Dwarka presents archaeologists with a real problem. Based on the dating of its age, this watery metropolis is, at the very least, some 5000 years older than any other civilizations anywhere in the world. This surprised archaeologists. They do think, however, the city came to be submerged as the result of the melting of the continental glaciers. And the name "Dwarka" is derived from the name of a legendary city, one that was said to belong to none other than Krishna, the Hindu God. Legends say that city sank beneath the waves, too.

8. **Helike.** Yet another ancient Greek metropolis, and this one was said to have sunk overnight. This occurred near the end of 373 BCE. Situated in Achaea, in the northern Peloponnese, the city was situated just about a mile from the shores of the Corinthian Gulf. Although there are references to the city in Greek history, most archaeologists thought the place was just a legend. Then, in 2001, ruins were found in the Helike Delta. Dora Katsonopoulou, a Greek archaeologist decided the area was worth exploring more closely. As a result, more ruins were discovered.

There are more sunken cities, but this makes our point. There are many more such examples, instances of cities on the coastlines of northern Europe and elsewhere that have been drowned with the passing of time. Therefore, the idea of sunken cities is not only real, but has many reality-based examples to support it.

That the world sea levels rose over the last thousands of years is no longer denied. This rising of the sea level is due to the melting of the continental glaciers, and the retreat of the polar ice caps. Most scientists think it was more of a gradual process, or just had some intermittent small deluges. They claim the Black Sea, or the enlarging of it, may be result of one such deluge. The Black Sea was originally thought to be fresh water, or at least brackish. At some point in its history, the sea broke through the Straits of the Dardanelles and the Black Sea rose in size and salinity. Settlements drowned. There is actual evidence of these settlements underneath the Black Sea, so this idea really isn't in question, either.

In addition, some cities, especially around the Mediterranean, seem to have been the victim of earthquakes, and many of those sank "overnight" or without much warning. This, too, seems a fact. It is interesting to note how quickly such cities became lost to history, became mere "legends and myths" as many archaeologists once thought of them, only to recently find they did exist. Could we say the same for Atlantis?

Furthermore, many historians and archaeologists think the Black Sea flooding event may have been the trigger for what seems a racial memory of the Great Flood. Well, it might have for that specific region, but this still doesn't account for the fact that legends of the Great Flood are worldwide. Additionally, tales about the Great Flood from around the world are quite consistent in their details in many respects. The Chinese legend of the deluge has their version of a Noah. Native Americans do, as well.

Whether a boat, an ark, a raft or whatever, there always seems to be some version of a Noah, a great flood, and a means of surviving it for one particular family or small group of people and/or their animals. Moreover, the stories all say the Great Flood happened quickly. Could this be true and the archaeologists wrong? Could the Great Flood have happened over a relatively short duration? Alternatively, might at least part of it have happened this way, instead of taking decades, or even centuries to raise the level of the world's oceans? It is a distinct possibility, as we shall see in a later chapter.

CHAPTER 9

LOST CIVILIZATIONS OF

ANTIQUITY

The idea of one civilization has always stayed prevalent in our history, even as individual empires rose and fell, but with a general upward trend in technologies is only partially true. Civilizations, as a whole, can and do expire, leaving little behind them. They are then sometimes completely forgotten. Whatever technologies they might have had also seem often to die with them.

Why is this topic important here? Because it shows that in the long sweep of history, entire civilizations can vanish from our memory, and much more often than people might think. In addition, this isn't just because they were city-states and happened to sink beneath the waves due to earthquakes.

Besides sunken cities, we also have lost civilizations on land, as well. Something happened to them, and archaeologists, for the most part, often simply don't know what. In many cases, they weren't even aware such civilizations had existed, even until very recently. Satellite maps have indicated the existence of some of these:

1. Rama Empire. Little is known about this ancient empire, except through the vedic texts of India. This civilization is far older and so advanced that it has left many archaeologists scratching their heads in wonder and frustration, as well. One thing is certain, the uncovering of the cities of Mohenjo-Daro and Harappa has already rewritten the timeline for archaeologists, like it or not. Originally, civilization in the Indus Valley region of India was thought to have started around 500 BCE.

With the discovery and recent greater excavations of the ruins of these two cities, this idea of 500 BCE now is gone of necessity, because it seems civilization in the area started thousands of years earlier. Harappa and Mohenjo-Daro were planned cities it seems, to the point where Mohenjo-Daro is almost monotonous in its grid system (think New York).

Besides this, the city had sewer systems and even indoor plumbing! The planning of the cities shows they must have been "preplanned" as archaeologists put it. This means the cities were sited, designed and then deliberately built. They were constructed for some deliberate purpose, which is strange in itself, because no other civilization then, or much later, seems to have done this. Yes, certain structures were built on purpose in later cities, such as palaces and walls, of course, but not entire, preplanned cities.

The cities of the Rama Empire were oddly preplanned, because they were "classless." No provision for the wealthy and powerful seems to have been made in any way in these cities. There were no "better" dwellings, special palaces, etc. There were even wide walks with drainage at either side to keep the roads clear of excess water.

Did the Rama Empire have a classless society? Possibly, or possibly these cities were all built for one class alone, as we have done in recent times when large construction projects require laborers to relocate to "temporary" cities nearby, as with the Hoover-Boulder Dam construction.

At its peak, the Rama Empire may have had a population around five million people. This is no small number, for it alone would then have accounted for one-tenth of the entire population of the planet at the time, according to reliable estimates. The empire was vast, even by today's standards, including major portions of India, Afghanistan, Iran, and Pakistan. Many buildings had more than one story and there was metalworking, because shops devoted to this specialty have been found, as well as other types of shops, as well.

Although some archaeologists speculate a change in weather, a lack of rain may have contributed to the abandonment of the cities, it's hard to imagine such a vast region would have been abandoned, stretching from Iran to India. Even now, despite extensive desertification, there are still good-sized populations in these regions. Moreover, conditions then were certainly wetter than they are now. Besides which, many of the cities were built along rivers.

Whatever happened to the Rama Empire must have been a very complete sort of event, since nobody today knows anything about the empire at all. This last, in itself is yet one more of countless enigmas with regard to the Rama Empire. Again, we have no knowledge of the language, writing, or the people. Yet, the planning of such cities had to require some sort of writing and good mathematical skills to lay out such geometrically perfect cities.

Such preplanning, such precision, such lack of better buildings for the rich than the poor flies in the face of everything archaeologists have ever known about cities and city-states of ancient times, and even the vast majority of cities on Earth today. No other civilization known in our ancient past or even more recently, ever built in such a way.

In fact, quite the opposite is true. Most cities are "organic," and seem to grow and change as needed. Not those of the Rama Empire. One thing seems certain; when the cities were abandoned, it was because they were destroyed. This doesn't sound as if it was changing weather patterns then, as the cause, but rather a great war of some type. Extensive ash layers and burned ruins supply convincing evidence for this idea at Mohenjo-Daro.

However, so long ago was all this, that in the intervening time much has been lost in the way of knowledge, especially of this Harappa or Rama Empire culture. Truly, the Rama Empire, of which the vedic texts say that Harappa and Mohenjo-Daro were only a part, is an enigma of the first order.

2. **Puma Punku And Tiwanaku.** Yes, most of us have heard of these two sites, situated so close together, but they do bear mentioning, if only in brief, because of recently revised estimates of their age, making them considerably older than originally thought.

Not a city, Puma Punku is composed of the remains of four buildings. Despite much controversy about the age of the buildings in the past, the general opinion is that they now date back close to 15,000 years in age. This makes them older than the Egyptian pyramids, and presents us with another mystery. Nobody seems to know who could have made them.

According to all current archaeological theories, no known civilization in the Americas that dates back so far, or would be capable in any way of creating such advanced structures. However the blocks were cut, the so-called H-blocks, for instance (because they look like a capital "H" in design), the methods used were so precise they would be hard to achieve even today. They have a decidedly "machined" look to them.

Besides the structures, there is extensive evidence of sewage lines, an irrigation system, and even methods for moving water in the area. How anyone had such capabilities so very long ago is a real question, and another of those major enigmas, because there is absolutely no evidence to explain who or what the builders might have been.

As a side note, due to the disarray of the blocks, some archaeologists think this was a result of a flood, perhaps occurring because of a meteor impact or some such thing in nearby Lake Titicaca. However, might this be part of the Great Flood evidence? If so, the flood extended to a much higher altitude than originally thought, because this area is at an altitude of approximately 3962 meters.

This seems incredibly high, even for the Great Flood, but it would explain why all the stories of the flood speak of survivors and even arks finding refuge on only the highest mountains, that even hills weren't safe from the waters. This also might mean the Great Flood might have been in the nature of a tsunami, although to have one reach so high would have required a very powerful meteor or asteroid impact, or one very close to the coastlines.

There is yet another strange oddity about Puma Punku, but not just it alone. This one also includes Korichancha, as well as Egypt, and a couple of other locations. It seems metal inserts or "clamps" to hold stones together were used as part of the construction process. These clamps were not made and then placed in the carved grooves for the purpose, but instead, after careful examination, it has been determined the metal had been poured into them, the metal still being molten, in a liquid state.

This is yet one more enigma, because:

a. Accomplishing this feat would require portable smelters, and this for a people who lived 15,000 years ago, some 10,000 years before our recorded civilization began.

b. The types of metal used required very high temperatures, ones that such a people should have been absolutely incapable of achieving!

c. The fact these clamps can be found at different places, including Korichancha and Yurock Rumi, as well as in Egypt, means the knowledge was widespread. In other words, it seems to have been worldwide, too.

Yet, in the ensuing several centuries, this knowledge seems to have been utterly lost, vanished without a trace, even as the builders of Puma Punku vanished. How can we account for this, a high level of technology that subsequently vanishes just a few centuries later to the point of not even being remembered at all, unless something catastrophic happened?

Since this catastrophe must have occurred in the New World, as well as the Old, because the knowledge was in both locations and disappeared from both, whatever happened had to have been on a large scale.

There is final thing to mention; there is no evidence of any forerunner development of this specialized knowledge. No smelters or other types of clamps, less advanced ones, for instance, have been found in any of these areas. It's as if the knowledge just popped into existence as to how to do this, and then disappeared again just as thoroughly, and just a few centuries later, at most.

3. **Lost Civilization in the Amazon**. According to *National Geographic News*, extensive ruins have been found in cleared areas of the rain forests of South America. The ruins, now merely raised mounds in the earth (earthworks), are in the shapes of squares, circles, triangles, and more. Satellite images of the area, taken since 1999, show over 200 such ruins. This, in itself, would be a startling discovery, but more was to come. More recent satellite photos show other structures in the rainforests themselves, and hint at even yet more, possibly ten times as many, as have already been discovered so far.

The most astonishing fact of all is these ruins, scattered about as they are, they could well cover an area greater than Texas! Archaeologists had always thought the land was too poor to support such a complex culture, one that may well date back to the time of Christ or perhaps even earlier.

Why is this important if it is not an old enough civilization to really be included in ones that date back 10,000 to 12,000 years ago? Because this discovery shows the severe limitations of archaeologists. These earthworks, so extensive in size and number, were only discovered in the last two decades. The question has to be asked, what else are archaeologists missing, and what else are they getting wrong? If a civilization that spanned an area the size of Texas is completely unknown to us, are there other such disappeared civilizations we have yet to find, as well?

Furthermore, nobody seems to have any idea what civilization created this Texas-sized region of earthworks and ruins. Almost nothing is known about the builders. So who were the builders? Why did they vanish? Had they cleared the forests only to have them encroach again after they had disappeared as a civilization, as is happening with the Mayan ruins of the Central American region? There are many questions about these people, and to date, almost no answers. They are truly a lost civilization.

4. **Catalhöyük.** This city is bizarre by any standards, because it isn't just an ancient city, but rather a "city building." The metropolis was one vast building, for there were no roads within it. Dating back to around 11,000 years ago, Catalhöyük was in Turkey and was built in a "hive-like" way. Based on an agrarian society that grew wheat as well as other crops, the only way for inhabitants to enter their dwellings was via ladders through holes in the roofs. Although not seeming to have a written language as such, they did have art and left various images behind for us to see. Nor was this a small town by the standards of the day. The city may have contained as many as 10,000 people!

Like so many of these ancient civilizations, at some point, the inhabitants simply seemed to have abandoned it. The cause is unknown, however, there is no evidence it was due to invaders or destruction. As with most of these mysterious civilizations, there are some incredible oddities. For example, they buried their dead beneath the dirt-packed floors of the homes. Another oddity is that quite a number of people might live in a home, but in most cases, they were not related! Families, as we think of them, apparently did not exist in this city building.

5. **Nan Madol.** This is another of those unaccountable discoveries. In the islands of Micronesia is a small island call Pohnpei. Here, is what amounts to a small ancient city built right on top of a coral reef. It is old, very old and seems to have been there before the seas rose. The structures themselves

are of basalt with some of the stone blocks weighing up to fifty tons. There are many canals running through the city, as well as tunnels, although these are now below water and so, impassable without the proper diving gear.

Nan Madol is no small feat. It has been compared to the Pyramids of Giza for effort, although the blocks don't weigh as much, being only three tons or so, on average. Built around 200 BCE, nobody has any idea of just who the builders were.

Furthermore, nobody can even explain where the basalt came from, since this is a coral island with no such material on it. Who the builders were, their purpose, the source of the building materials, how they managed to transport them, is all a mystery. Even how they managed to place the blocks on top of each other to a height of 15.24 meters is a complete enigma. One other strange thing; the bones found dating back to that time are not like the bones of the present day inhabitants of the island, for they are much larger. One report even says, "remarkably larger."

Nan Midol is one of the more perplexing lost civilization mysteries, because nobody even knows why they wanted to go through such effort to build the city where they did. Again, nothing about the city is clear. Even finding out where the basalt blocks came from would be a help, because again, such material certainly isn't indigenous to that area at all.

Therefore, in conclusion of this chapter, we see that not only do civilizations vanish beneath the waves, but also on land, as well. This lends credence to the idea that if so many civilizations can be forgotten to the point of virtual nonexistence, then it also seems reasonable to think that such may have happened with a larger civilization, a worldwide one. This could be especially true if:

1. Thousands of years had passed since the civilization collapsed.

2. Some great catastrophe or catastrophes caused its destruction and so, together with extreme age and erosion, wiped out much of the remains of such a civilization.

3. The civilization in question was never large in population numbers to begin with, so its physical "footprint" in locations around the world wasn't big.

Civilizations vanish. Did a worldwide one of "others," meaning non-humans do this? We need more pieces of the puzzle, more evidence to find out. As it so happens, there is more in the way of evidence.

PART THREE

THE "PRE-ADAMITES"

Prior To 10,000 BCE   10,000 BCE 3500 BCE 2015 CE

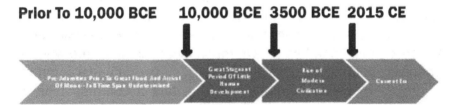

**Great Flood Triggered
By Arrival of Moon**

Figure 3 Timeline: Pre-Adamite Civilization, Time Span In Tens Of Thousands Of Years. This Ends With Moon's Arrival And Resulting Great Flood In 10,000 BCE (12,000 Years Ago), Followed By Great Stagnant Period Of 6500 Years Before Rise of Modern Civilization At 5500 years ago.

CHAPTER 10

EVIDENCE FOR "PRE-ADAMITES"

We have discussed many things up until this point. Included in this, were the so-called "ooparts," vanished civilizations, sunken cities, and more. We have also established that civilization seems to have been around a lot longer than our current one is supposed to have been, and some civilizations have come and gone, sometimes leaving almost no trace of their having been. Moreover, this book has shown much evidence of a time when a worldwide culture, a global civilization of sorts that had a common writing, perhaps a common language, and a common type of architecture existed.

We've also talked about giants in depth. Specifically, we talked about whether they actually existed or not. It seems some did. Their numbers never seem to have been large, but then given their size they didn't need to be. Giants do seem to have stridden the earth at one time, and on all continents. Evidence comes down to us in the form of extra-large skeletons, oversized skulls, skulls without sutures in them (at least, not as many as we humans have), and even evidence from written records of ancient times.

Even so, it seems giants, also known as the Nephilim, or the "Watchers," weren't the only people on Earth. In this chapter, I will provide some evidence for the fact of there being other species, as well. Later on, we'll discuss just what happened to them. Judging by all the evidence given here so far, whatever it was seems to have taken place around 10,000 BCE.

Nevertheless, let's look at what we can find out about the Pre-Adamites themselves before such an event occurred and see if they actually existed. Do we have evidence to support this idea? Yes, it would seem we do.

We have already spoken of the World Map Stone, that ancient object which seems to depict Atlantis in the center of the Atlantic Ocean. If one looks at the image of the stone carefully, one can readily see that Atlantis seems to have been situated with at least part of it over the Mid-Atlantic Ridge. This, in itself, is an intriguing bit of evidence, because the Mid-Atlantic Ridge is an extremely active geological zone. This ridge runs north and south almost all the way up and down the Atlantic Ocean. Near its northern tip is Iceland. As most of us know, Iceland is incredibly geologically active. Earth tremors proliferate there. Multiple volcanoes exist, and they cause serious problems all the time.

Devastating volcanic eruptions occur often. As recently as 2010, air-traffic all over Western Europe and even parts of the United States was interfered with, because of the ash clouds produced by an erupting volcano. Much of the land in Iceland is relatively new, constantly formed from lava and pyroclastic flows. Although many Icelanders might resent it, one has to say that Iceland is not a very safe place to live because of all this fiery geological activity. Moreover, volcanoes don't stop at the shoreline. There are subterranean volcanoes and geological fissures all up and down the Mid-Atlantic Ridge.

If Atlantis straddled this ridge, then it must have suffered from much the same sort of problems, geologically speaking, as Iceland does now. In short, it seems Atlantis might not have been a very stable place to live, either. Under normal circumstances, this might have been an acceptable risk for the people of Atlantis. However, if a large planetary-wide catastrophe occurred, then all bets might have been off.

The problem with such a catastrophe occurring, especially if it was on a global scale, is that it tends to wipe out a lot of the evidence one might otherwise have available to us modern humans. Then, too, remember that continental glaciers covered large parts of the Earth. Although these were in retreat, they still covered truly vast areas of land. Besides this, then the sea levels rose and so water covered much of the land. One way or the other, things were hidden.

Humans tend to live along coastal regions, and at the confluences of rivers or near river deltas. The reason for this is simple. Often, the land is flat at, or near the coastline, although of course, in some cases not. However, having cities built on the coast, especially on bays and inlets, makes for very good trade and commerce capabilities. Moreover, the often more level land there is better for agriculture. River deltas, for instance, although very fertile regions for crops, are very flat and close to existing sea levels in altitude.

This means, with the major flooding caused by the end of the glacial period, a lot more evidence was submerged or destroyed. Necessarily then, we are left with just bits and pieces, scraps of writing, and a few of the more lasting types of evidence, such as stone monuments. Yet, this doesn't mean we don't have any evidence at all. We do.

Furthermore, we have something else. The Pre-Adamites seem to have been revered by us lesser humans. They were often referred to as gods, demigods, and more. This helps, because those places frequented by the Pre-Adamites were special to humans as a result. We revered them. They became so-called sacred places. Some still are considered such today. The Baalbek platform is one. For ages, one civilization after another built their sacred temples on what they felt had long been a holy site, since time immemorial, in fact.

Baalbek is named for the god, Baal, but later the Greeks built temples there, and after them, so did the Romans. The same seems to hold true for The Temple of the Mount in Jerusalem. This site, too, has held special religious significance since prehistory. Furthermore, the same thing has happened there, with various religions claiming the privilege of building their holy structures on the supposed sacred site.

Please note that the Temple of the Mount platform or foundation has always been far larger than any human structure built on it, so whoever originally built the platform seems to have had something else in mind, something other than just a mosque or temple.

The point here is that one way of spotting ancient sites of the Pre-Adamites is at least to partly focus on such long-term, "sacred" sites. Those with a long history of being holy probably were places of the Pre-Adamites, and not just in the Middle East, but also around the world. Wherever the gods gathered, it seemed, a special holiness attached itself to that area. Even though the exact reason for why a place is considered holy is often lost over time, the "holiness" of the location, the belief in the sacred aspect of the area, remains.

Therefore, besides having stone monuments, writings, bones, and such, we also have the sacred sites. What's more, we have many written records that talk about these Pre-Adamites. Remember, we use this term somewhat loosely—"Pre-Adamites." Pre-Adamite, again, means "before Adam," but this does not mean they disappeared with the arrival of Adam, or of our first human ancestors. It merely means they predated us.

There seems to be evidence, which we will go into further depth in the next chapter, that humans and Pre-Adamites coexisted for a long time, that they had a strong impact on us, our culture, our society, and yes, even our religions. Many researchers think they are the original foundation for our religions of today. These researchers say the first servants in the temples of the gods were just that, servants. They waited on the so-called gods, literally. Being the most trusted of humans, they were granted special status and privileges, just as other humans were, as well, for doing other services to the gods, as with the human pilots of some of the vimanas, those flying vehicles of the ancient gods, as referred to in the Hindu vedic texts.

So in the opinion of these researchers today, our current priests of churches and temples are still trying to fulfill the function of serving their god or gods, even though, again according to these researchers, the gods have long since vanished from this Earth. It is almost as if the servants are still maintaining the palaces of their disappeared masters, and this is a rather chilling idea, I think, but possibly a true one.

CHAPTER 11

THE "PRE-ADAMITES"—

BUILDING A PICTURE

We have gone back from our current time, to that of ancient civilization. We have passed the beginnings of this at around 3500 BCE. Going still further into the past we entered the era of the first dark ages, that long period of 6500 years I referred to as the Stagnant Period of humanity. This is when archaeologists and historians say humans lived in small communities. They were basic agrarian settlements or groups of hunters and gatherers. These people were mere tribes of necessity. They never were in very large numbers.

As mentioned before in this book, this is not a time of architecture, construction projects, or much of anything else. It was as if, somehow, humans were marking time. In any case, then we moved even back further on our timeline, to around 10,000 BCE. This puts us at about 12,000 years ago.

Here, things seem to have been different. However, how different?

1. Based on evidence from around the world, we have construction going on before 10,000 BCE. "Megaliths," as archaeologists like to call them, had gone up around the world. They are all similar in nature, hewn from stone or made of stone blocks in some way. There are circles, as well as lines of seemingly endless stone monuments. Whether we are talking about Göbekli Tepe, the Platform of Baalbek in Lebanon, the Temple of the Mount Platform, the Sphinx, the Pyramids of Giza, pyramids found around the world, the ancient constructions of China, Bolivia, or wherever, there is evidence of very ancient stone structures being built on a worldwide basis.

2. Some of the structures were constructed so long ago that sea level rises have inundated many of them. The Yoniguni Pyramid in Japan is just one example of a submerged site. There are many more.

Therefore, we have established that around 10,000 BCE, someone was building huge stone structures utilizing types of methods we can't even determine today. We do know some of them seem to be even beyond our present day capabilities. Moreover, we have no idea what many of these stone structures were for originally.

Why, for example, would such huge platforms, meters upon meters thick, with stones weighing so much, be used as a simple foundation for the later building of temples that were but a fraction in size compared to the massive platform itself? It doesn't make logical sense. In addition, evidence indicates these platforms were millennia before such temples to Baal, or later Jupiter, were constructed on them. So if not temples, for what were they constructed?

We can only make general surmises in this regard. Some may be spot on, but others may be way off, as a result. Debate over the reason for the construction of the Pyramids of Giza, for example, rages on. Mainstream archaeologists say these giant pyramids were tombs for pharaohs. However, we have no real evidence of them really being any such thing at all.

No hieroglyphics pertaining to any service funerary rites, the interment of any particular pharaohs, or anyone for that matter, have been found inside these pyramids. The pyramids are absent of hieroglyphics of any sort, which is very strange. No mummies have been found there. No funerary equipment has been discovered in any of them. Therefore, the idea the Pyramids of Giza were giant tombs for ancient kings in Egypt really is just a matter of conjecture and truly nothing more.

Whatever this civilization was, it seems to have had some type of written language. The markings on the World Map Stone are just too similar in nature to markings found elsewhere around the planet. Besides this, we have incredibly similar symbols, such as the swastika, and the spiral showing up in various places around the world. Always, no matter where found, these markings seem to have some sort of religious overtones to them and the question has to be, is this merely some massive coincidence, or is there something more to all this?

The answer, of course, is that such a coincidence on a global scale and in hundreds if not thousands of places, can hardly be a coincidence. There has to be some universal or overriding connection that ties these things all together.

Therefore, we can conclude the Pre-Adamites were workers in stone. They built on large scales, and had a predilection for pyramids and monuments. They had a written language and symbolism. In addition, if the ancient mines of South Africa are anything to go by, they also had metallurgy, as well. Gold seemed to be particularly popular, but copper, tin, iron, and other metals were also mined far back before 10,000 BCE.

So unlike most archaeologists who think civilization didn't arise until thousands of years later, it would seem there was quite a thriving one some 6500 years earlier than those researchers believe. Moreover, as with so much else in the way of evidence in this book, these pieces of evidence all date back to around 12,000 years ago or more. However, the cutoff date for them, in the main, seems to have been around 10,000 BCE, or again, 12,000 years ago.

As intriguing as all this is about the distinct probability of a world culture in so ancient a time, the question remains if there is any way we can know more about these people. There is so little to go on after so long a time, with weathering and erosion having had 10,000 years to wipe out much of what might have survived otherwise. If I stress this point here, it is because so many ask where all the evidence for such a culture is? Well, how much of our civilization would last 10,000 years, even without catastrophic events occurring? The answer may surprise you.

Modern civilization would leave almost nothing of itself in just a few thousand years if all our works were suddenly abandoned. Vehicles would rust to dust and blow away. Skyscrapers would crumble to powder. Our vast freeway systems would bend, break, crack, and buckle, then eventually erode away to nothing. Native vegetation would return, with roots and plants further cracking and breaking up any ruins left behind. Rain, wind, sunlight, would do continuous damage, as well.

As much as eco-minded citizens decry the use of plastics, it is a certainty no plastics would survive for 10,000 years, not even in landfills. Plastic, although long lasting, simply isn't forever. Neither is glass. Being in reality a super cooled-liquid, glass is actually flowing, if extremely slowly, all the time. Take a windowpane from a long abandoned house and measure the thickness of the top of the pane against the bottom, and one can readily see the top is thinner. Gravity is causing the seemingly solid glass to slowly flow downwards. Eventually, the pane becomes a puddle. Again, wind, rain, and erosion would turn that glass back into sand and dust.

Sadly, the ruins of our civilization wouldn't last as long as the ruins of ancient Rome have done, as it turns out. The Romans used a better concrete than we do. Therefore, their ruins have lasted longer than ours would under similar circumstances.

What else could we go by? Perhaps we could find lingering radiation from our nuclear power plants? Not likely. Over the course of 10,000 years, the half-life of the various isotopes used for nuclear fuel and the resulting radioactive byproducts would cause such materials to lose their radioactivity. Even strontium 90, one of the most feared radioactive products of a nuclear blast because of its relative longevity, only has a half-life of 28.8 years. This means that in just twenty-nine years after a thermonuclear blast, half the strontium 90 would be gone. In another twenty-nine years, half of the remaining amount would then be gone, as well, and so on, until there was virtually nothing left. This may be long in the terms of one person's lifetime, but it is nothing compared to ten millennia!

Why is a point made of all this about the non-durability of our current civilization? Because 10,000 years is a long time! When critics of the idea of a world civilization having once existed long ago claim there is little evidence for such a thing, the answer has to be, of course not! Not after 10,000 years. Yet amazingly, there does seem to be a lot of evidence. We are lucky in that the ancients chose stone as their durable building material, rather than the cheaper and weaker concrete we use today, a material that even the ancient Romans disdained from using as being too inferior in quality.

Moreover, besides such physical remains of an extinct civilization, there are the written records of our various cultures and civilizations around the world that can give us an inkling of what the Pre-Adamites might have been like. For one thing, they seem to have been much taller than we are. By our standards, they were truly giants.

Whether we refer to them as the Nephilim, the Watchers, or just "giants of old," they seem to have been, generally, much taller and larger than we are. Based on the various stories and evidence, the average height was about 2.43 meters or a little more. Since some humans have reached this height, this is hardly impossible. Skeletal remains and stories from such diverse cultures as the Hebrew, and North American natives, all say pretty much the same thing, as well. There is a continuity of the details of tales about giants from around the world.

We may also consider the fact humans seem to have existed back then, too. Again, evidence suggests that just as with the Pre-Adamites, our numbers were not large. However, we did exist then. Archaeological records of human remains show this to be a fact.

Therefore, it seems we existed in the same world as the giants did, but we were not on the same level, it would seem. All stories tell, in some way or other, of the power of the giants, versus our weakness compared to them. Therefore, it is eminently reasonable to assume they dominated us.

Again, we have the records of the Sumerians, which explicitly tell us this. They tell us we were servants to the Anunnaki. They also say we had no choice in the matter. In addition, they say an intriguing thing more, and that is, they created us for just that purpose—to serve. Whether or not we were, I cannot say for sure. However, there is some intriguing evidence that this could well have been the case. We'll discuss that a little later on this book.

Humans Bred with some Unknown Species. Recent analysis in England of ancient DNA has shocked the archaeological community. According to the findings, human ancestors interbred with a totally unknown species at one point, and one that existed about 30,000 years ago. This species seems to have come from Asia, but researchers have determined it was not Neanderthals but a seemingly different species. Again, what species this might have been is totally unknown to modern science. This is besides our later interbreeding with Neanderthals.

There is much debate among researchers as to just who or what this species might have been. There just isn't enough available evidence at this point to have any real idea. Scientists merely refer to them as the "mystery species." A mystery, they are. However, there are clear traces of the unknown species and their strange genome in the skeletal remains of a Denisovan human, found in a cavern in eastern (Siberia) Russia.

Again, nothing is known about who this species was, but this is more evidence we have abrupt and strange changes in the genome or our human ancestors. Just as with the sudden change of 4500 years ago from dark-skinned and light-eyed Europeans to suddenly become light-skinned and light-eyed ones, here we have further evidence of tampering, either inadvertent or perhaps deliberate with the human species as we know it today.

Elongated Skulls. Elongated skulls may have been the norm for the giants of old. Elongated skulls come from around the world.

Most of these were the result of people purposely deforming their children's skulls by using wooden boards strapped to the baby's head to force the skulls into a different shape.

However, many ancient alien theorists believe this was in imitation of those "giants of old" who had such skulls. We see evidence for this imitation not just in the deforming process of many people's head around the world this way (meaning it was a worldwide phenomenon), but also in the types of helmets and crowns worn by rulers of various empires, such as the Pharaohs of Egypt, Assyria, etc. It is said, "Imitation is the sincerest form of flattery." It seems to have been with many rulers in many lands. They borrowed the look of the Pre-Adamites, perhaps, to help instill the idea of their natural right to rule. Many rulers went even further, and along with such headgear, proclaimed themselves, divine, as well. This, too, was probably in imitation of the Pre-Adamites who ruled in antediluvian times, those "demigods."

Please note, not all elongated skulls were a result of deliberate deformations. Skulls have been found that defy this explanation, and in plenty. For instance, in Paracas, Peru, a major discovery was made in 1928. Julia Tello, an archaeologist, discovered a very complete cemetery. The tombs and graveyard, when unearthed, had many skeletons with elongated heads. The archaeologist, at first assumed these were the result of purposeful deformation, as so many other such finds had been. These turned out to be quite different. Over 300 skulls were elongated, but they weren't the result of deformation. The so-called "Paracas skulls" as they came to be known, dated back close to 1000 BCE or more.

Furthermore, in recent days, a full DNA analysis and tests were done for one of the skulls. Contrary to showing the skulls had been deformed by binding, which doesn't alter the actual size of skulls, or the overall weight, the tests clearly showed the elongated skull had a greater brain capacity, some twenty-five percent more than standard human skulls did. The thing was heavier, as well as thicker. Another oddity is there was only one suture rather than two sutures, as is the norm for human children. Sutures are areas of the skull that at one time weren't joined, allowing the baby's brain to grow. As time passes, these different plates merge and a so-called suture line is formed where they fuse.

The problem seems to be, if not the result of deliberate deformation, how did these elongated skulls come about? How did beings achieve a greater cranial capacity, a thicker skull, a heavier one, and not have as many parietal plates? If this was a mutation, it wasn't just one, but a whole set of them. Or, the skulls were not quite human...

Given the fact deformation was worldwide, but done to humans, that rulers of many lands imitated the elongated head by the shape of their crowns, and the fact skulls have been found, ones which don't appear to be entirely human, it would be a reasonable assumption that many, if not all of the Nephilim or Anunnaki had elongated skulls. So not only were they giants in comparison to the average human of the time, but they had oddly shaped elongated heads, ones with a higher cranial capacity than us.

Our picture of the Pre-Adamites is getting clearer. In addition, we can know about them more. For example, these giants also seemed to have been possessed of long lives, which would have been another great advantage over us normal humans. Various tales and legends of the Middle East, written records from the Babylonians, the Sumerians, and even the Old Testament, speak of people of those times as being capable of many wonders. No wonder, they created the Platform of Baalbek, the Jerusalem Temple of the Mount, the Pyramids of Giza, and the Sphinx. Yes, mainstream archaeologists think the pyramids are much younger, but there are also mainstream archaeologists and researchers who think otherwise, that the structures are far older. Given the evidence presented earlier in this book, they may well be right.

The worldwide civilization of the Pre-Adamites had a lot going for it. Being global, they had had some system of global communications and commerce. Shipping would seem to be the obvious way of them conducting their communications, etc. However, do remember that this far back in time, there was more land area and less ocean area. There were land bridges between many places. Australia wasn't isolated at that time. Great Britain was still connected to the European continent. Travel and commerce would have been easier.

Were Pre-Adamites Here For Ages? The *Sumerian Kings List* was a very strange find. Several versions of this list have been discovered, some more complete than others were. So far, the most all-inclusion version discovered now resides in England.

The interesting thing about the *Sumerian Kings List*, is just how far back it goes. According to the ancient Sumerians, the list includes a number of kings who reigned prior to the Great Flood, of which the list speaks. As mentioned before, these kings ruled by a divine right, or were considered divine. One of the reasons for this idea is the number of years some of those kings are said to have lived, according to the *Kings List*. The antediluvian kings didn't just reign for centuries, but in some instances, are said to have reigned for thousands of years! Moreover, the Kings List says their right to rule, their kingships, "had descended from heaven."

Again, we have that reference to an otherworldly source for the powers and rights of these "divine" kings with the very origin of the concept of kingship, which is seen as a divine institution, "descending from heaven," perhaps, quite literally. The list starts with the first king, and this was in Eridug of Sumeria. A fellow by the name of Alulim ruled a very long time, or as the Kings List says:

"He ruled for 28,800 years. Alaljar ruled for 36,000 years. Two kings; they ruled for 64,800 years."

These kings made people like Methuselah and Noah look like mere infants by comparison to their extreme age. *The Kings List* includes eight such long-lived kings, who combined, reigned for a total of 241,200 years, if the *Kings List* is to be believed. These were all that ruled, or apparently needed to rule, since they lived so long, until the time of the "the Flood." After this, according to the *Kings List,* "the kingship was lowered from heaven" after the Flood, meaning the connection was broken.

This sounds amazingly as if the Pre-Adamites, those incredibly long-lived "giants" with elongated heads, had vanished, and humans then took over the kingship in their stead, but humans weren't long lived. So there are a lot of human kings on the list after the Flood.

Of course, this has raised all sorts of questions in the archaeological community with debates and opinions raging on all sides. One can run the entire gamut from the *Kings List* just being a thing of pure fiction, to those who are convinced it may be telling the literal truth, that the antediluvian kings were something other than standard humans.

It should be noted that there does seem to be a correlation between many aspects of the *Kings List* and the Book of Genesis in the Bible. The Great Flood, for instance, is mentioned in both. And by odd coincidence or otherwise, despite the extreme age or lifespans of the Sumerian's kings, just eight generations passed between the first until the one of the Great Flood.

In the Bible, the same amount of time is noted, with their being just eight generations between Adam, and Noah. In addition, both the *Kings List* and Genesis mention not only the saving of certain individuals during the flood, but also of various types of animals. Again, this is highly coincidental, to say the least.

Those who claim the *Sumerian Kings List* deliberately combined mythical kingships with real ones are hard pressed to explain why the Sumerians would have bothered to do this. It is just one of the many enigmas surrounding the list. Additionally, nobody seems able to figure out why the lifespans of such ruler would have been deliberately distorted to such a tremendous degree, or why the Book of Genesis in the Bible has so many consistent similarities to the *Kings List*. It's all more than just a little bizarre

So what happened to the Pre-Adamites? What made them disappear? What led to a 6500 year interregnum after their disappearance? Oh, of course, we've been talking about the Great Flood. That event had a great deal to do with the demise of the Pre-Adamite culture. We will talk more about this later on.

Nevertheless, what triggered the Great Flood? What caused this sudden massive and worldwide deluge? Additionally, we need to ask from where the Pre-Adamites managed to obtain their civilization? The reason we must ask this is that we have no record of a gradual buildup to such a civilization. There is no long buried record of such a people slowly acquiring all these skills and knowledge. Yes, we have evidence of truly ancient mines, and other structures. We have the so-called ooparts, some of which seem to date back even millions of years. However, these last are oddities; they are the exceptions and not the rule. There is no distinct layer of earth we've discovered with debris and/or artifacts of the Pre-Adamites.

Therefore, we have to assume that the Pre-Adamites somehow obtained their culture from elsewhere, and either:

1. The same source, as it was the same worldwide culture, but also,

2. At the same time. This is because we don't have an archaeological record of much else other than their stone monuments, pyramids, platforms, and such. The Pre-Adamite culture seems to have somehow already been at its peak when it died, and there was no build-up to this peaking, as far as we can tell. They just "were always there," so to speak, complete with their technology, and all at once.

Now we are left with two major questions:

1. From where did the Pre-Adamites come? Were they always here, or did they come from "somewhere" else?

2. What happened to destroy them? We survived the Great Flood, so why didn't they? After all, they lived longer, were more powerful, and seemingly had ruled for tens of thousands of years, or more.

These are two provocative questions, for which we really need answers. But is there any available evidence to help us with this? The answer is yes, we do have some evidence to aid us in answering these questions, as well.

CHAPTER 12

HOW LONG WERE THE

"PRE-ADAMITES" HERE?

This is a tough question to answer, because it is hard to estimate just how long the Pre-Adamites were on our world. This is because of a number of questions:

1. Were all the Pre-Adamites the same "people?"

2. Did they all arrive here at the same time?

3. Did all the Pre-Adamites exist on Earth at the same time?

4. If different species, how many such Pre-Adamite species where there?

Herein lies our problem, because these questions are hard to answer. For one thing, it all happened so long ago, and for another, so little evidence has survived the ages.

However, again, we do have a number of sources of information/ evidence we can fall back on.

1. The first is ooparts. As mentioned earlier, ooparts abound. There are LOTS of them, thousands, at least. Many of these out-of-place objects seem to date incredibly far back in time. It's almost as if there might have been successive waves or colonies of extraterrestrials that came to Earth over thousands, or as the ooparts seem to indicate, even millions of years. There are vehicle ruts (mentioned in more detail later on) in the Maltese Archipelago and in Turkey. These date very far back in time, for example. Items found embedded in solid coal date to even more primeval times. Ladles and hand bells that may be millions of years old raise some serious questions about just what has been going on here on Earth, and for just how long.

Nevertheless, if we take the ooparts, or at least some of them as real physical evidence, we are left with the disturbing fact that those from "out there," may have been here for an extended time, or at least have come and gone over lengthy periods in Earth's history. Because of different types of structures and objects found, the evidence would also seem to indicate it might have been more than one race involved in colonizing or visiting Earth.

Furthermore, we have the vedic texts, which state there were around 400 or more types of aliens or "demons" as they refer to them, and that these were all somehow involved in a great war at some final point in time.

Yet, the evidence can be so sketchy and minimal in some instances. Many will ask: shouldn't there be more? Shouldn't we have dug up more skeletons, for instance, and other items, as well, if aliens were out and about Planet Earth for so many countless years?

Yes, we probably should have. Still there may be good reasons why this hasn't been so. First, remember, it seems skeletons of giants and people with elongated heads have been discovered in places around the world, so some real evidence does seem to exist for a "strange" people having lived around the planet. Yet, we naturally want more evidence. Despite numerous ancient structures, accounts of giants and their skeletons, as well as skulls and such, we want more "proof."

Yet combined with ooparts and stone ruins found all over the planet, written records, and oral traditions, some would argue a good deal of evidence has been discovered and from multiple sources. Many researchers, and yes, some archaeologists, as well, say mainstream archaeologists simply refuse to revise their opinions about such discoveries, or simply ignore them and/or call them (in their thousands) hoaxes.

They have a point. The mainstream sciences, with the possible exception of quantum physics, seem very slow to want to alter their viewpoints, and this is as it should be. Better not to make a quantum leap, if it ends in jumping to confusion. Even so, as evidence keeps coming in, it is difficult for archaeologists to continue to claim that all of these finds are of no importance, just anomalies, or hoaxes. Although, they just might...such is the nature of intransigent scholars that they are loath to let go of their worldview, their viewpoint of how the world is or should be. Nobody likes their applecart upset to such a degree, because in the case of these learned men and women, it means much of what they've learned and taught is simply wrong. Such a thing destroys reputations.

2. A small population? Could this account for the lack of more evidence? Remember, stories about the Anunnaki of the Sumerians talk about these so-called gods or demigods as not being large in numbers. The Sumerian cuneiform writings even claim we were created to serve and labor for the gods, because of their few numbers and them not wanting to do the nastier work themselves. Therefore, if the aliens were never large in numbers, they would leave correspondingly less behind. It is advisable to remember that most of the gods of most cultures were not large in numbers. There are some exceptions to this, as in India. The Vedic texts say there were many demons/gods, but not all, by any means, lived on Earth. Moreover, the texts do not say they were large in numbers for each type, but just that there were many types.

Perhaps, aliens just couldn't exit a spaceship and stroll freely on our world? Perhaps the gravity is wrong, or the air, or the bacteria/viruses in it? Maybe they could only go out and about for limited times as a result? Any number of factors might have limited the extraterrestrials' freedom of movement about our world. This could be the reason they so heavily used their "vimanas" of so many shapes and sizes. Perhaps, they need their environments to be controlled.

3. The Great Flood, triggered by the arrival of the Moon (more on this later, as well), would have done much to wipe out a record of these ancient interlopers on our planet.

4. Maybe, our world wasn't being colonized, so much as exploited. Perhaps, Earth had good resources, which could be tapped, as with the evidence of truly ancient mines in South Africa, Utah, and elsewhere, but nobody wanted to colonize the Earth. Maybe, planets just aren't that easy to colonize for any number of reasons or incompatibilities with certain species. This could well be why the Anunnaki created human servants, if that is true. Perhaps, they needed proxies, surrogates to do the work for them, because they simply couldn't exist unprotected in our environment for long. It could well be we were just an outpost used for our resources, a galactic gas station, or supply center, as it were.

If any of this were so, then it would certainly account for a lack of more evidence with regard to their having been here. However, for myself, I think there is lots of evidence. Ooparts written records, oral traditions, the finding of countless mammoth stone monuments and ruins around the world, etc., all seem ample evidence of Pre-Adamites having not only been here, but having been here for a long time, if not in great numbers.

CHAPTER 13

THEY CAME FROM "OUT THERE"

Considering the nature of these Nephilim, Anunnaki, Watchers, or whatever name one uses to call them, and seeing the evidence of different historical records, we should be able to arrive at some conclusions about them. So what do we know so far? Well, to recap:

1. **They Were Tall, Hence the Term Giants.** Their height seems to have been at least 2.43 meters. We get this from various accounts in different historical texts, cuneiform writings of the Sumerians, the Christian Old Testament of the Bible, the Hebrew Bible, and the Ethiopian Bible with its Book of Enoch. Moreover, we have evidence for the extreme height of the Pre-Adamites from skeletal remains found in different places around the world.

2. **The Pre-Adamites Were Possessed of Long Lives.** Again, we have multiple sources to support this contention. The Old Testament of the Christian Bible, the Hebrew Bible, and the Sumerian List of Kings, and again the Book of Enoch of the Ethiopian Bible all attest to the fact these people could live the

better part of a millennium, or in some cases, even multiple millenniums.

3. **They Were Highly Intelligent.** Not one instance of a "stupid" Pre-Adamite ever seems to have been recorded by any culture. Always, they are spoken of as being possessed of special knowledge, and special abilities. They were more often than not rulers, considered demigods, or even gods for this reason. In addition, there are numerous stories of them giving knowledge to us lesser humans, sometimes at a great personal price for breaking the rules.

4. **The Pre-Adamites Were Strong, Much Stronger than the Average Human.** This is so, if the written records of the Middle East and elsewhere are to be believed. Their strength, it seems, was commensurate with their height and weight. This means the average human (like us) would have been at a severe disadvantage in any major conflict with them. It's safe to assume humans probably avoided doing this for the most part. The outcome of such a confrontation would be in little doubt. Even the story of David and Goliath, in the Bible, shows this, because it appears David is specially blessed to be able to defeat such a towering monster as Goliath, and the entire rest of the Hebrew army wanted nothing to do with such a confrontation. Thus, it was not the norm for this to happen.

5. **They Were the Dominant Species on Earth.** Based on Number 4 above, we can reasonably assume we were not the dominant species on the planet, not if the Nephilim/Anunnaki were about the place, as they seem to have been. We must have then been in a subservient position to them, by not only a logical chain of reasoning, but also because we have the evidence for this fact in the form of cuneiform writings, which tell us just how subservient a people we were to the Anunnaki/Nephilim.

Then, in addition, there are passages in the Indian vedic texts that seem to support this contention, as well, referring to humans as being literally servants to the gods in their temples-cum-palaces. Moreover, the cuneiform tablets weren't the only ones to record the Nephilim as the dominant people of their times. Again, we have the Hebrew, as well as the Christian Bibles to reinforce this idea.

So where did they come from, these Nephilim, or whatever we choose to call them? Well, again, we have many historical records that say they came from "elsewhere," or were descended from the gods (even were gods), or "the kingship came down from heaven" and so they became the rulers of humans.

6. **Demigod Pharaohs.** The Egyptian histories claim that very early pharaohs were demigods. As mentioned earlier, often, they were depicted in images as having elongated heads/skulls. Even the traditional helmet or crown of the pharaohs resembled this shape, and when later pharaohs wore the crown, it gave them, too, the appearance of having elongated heads, even as their forbears, the demigod pharaohs, supposedly had naturally.

7. **Were Some of the Early Egyptian Pharaohs "Alien Hybrids?"** This, on the face of it, would seem an implausible question—were the original pharaohs from somewhere else, or descended from those who were? Do we have evidence, besides depictions of such pharaohs as with elongated skulls, and Egyptian hieroglyphics to prove some Egyptian rulers were actually "different" than most of the later ones? In fact, there does seem to be some scientific evidence for this idea.

8. **DNA Evidence.** New evidence from recent genetic research by Assistant Professor, Stuart Fleischmann of the Swiss University, Cairo, Egypt, and his researchers has been posted in the publishing of a seven-year study. The findings, although not yet independently corroborated, are incredible. For one

thing, they show that the ancient Egyptians did interact with an advanced race or extraterrestrials.

Professor Fleischmann and his team claim there is clear scientific evidence of "willful genetic manipulation" of the genome of the early pharaohs of Egypt, the so-called demigod kings. Some researchers have actually gone so far as to claim this as "definitive" evidence.

The professor and his team took years to map the entire genomes of no less than nine pharaohs. Eight out of the nine genomes resulting were what could be described as "normal," but not the ninth. This genome belongs to none other than the Pharaoh, Akhenaten. This pharaoh reigned in the fourteenth century, BCE, and is known for not only being the father of the famous King Tut (Tutankhamen), but being the pharaoh who introduced the idea of a monotheistic religion, one god, the Sun God.

Professor Fleischmann had repeatedly run DNA tests on a sample of brain tissue from the mummy of the pharaoh, but also, as independent verification, on some bone samples, as well. Both sets of tests resulted in the same conclusions. One of these was the gene, CXPAC-5, which is instrumental in the growth of the cortex in the brain, was much more prevalent in the sample than is typically found by far.

This strongly indicates Akhenaten most likely had a greater "cranial capacity." This would have to be so in order to allow for a correspondingly bigger cortex. This would account for the depictions of his having an elongated skull.

If this were a mutation, it is an inexplicable one, because to date, we have found no mutations which would allow for our brains to mutate to such a larger size naturally. The conclusion then is that it probably wasn't natural, but was the result of some sort of genetic manipulation, the interference with the natural human genome in this regard. It should be mentioned, as well, that the pharaoh had other physical oddities about him, such as a protruding stomach, wide hips, etc., at least, if one goes by all the ancient engravings of his image.

However, if true, this means Akhenaten's genome was manipulated in some way. Nobody then living had anywhere near such capabilities. Even today, with all the advances we've made in genetics, we do not have the ability to alter the human brain to make it grow larger and so correspondingly more intelligent, because increased cranial capacity, in proportion to the body size of a creature, usually means just that—increased intelligence.

Furthermore, the pharaoh had a very low level of telomerase. This enzyme disappears over time in humans and animals as they age. Dolly, the cloned sheep, for example, was cloned from an aging parent. Dolly, the new offspring, had no more telomerase than her "parent" had. As a result, the sheep had to be put down at an earlier than normal age when it developed severe arthritis, a type associated with aging creatures. Akhenaten was only about forty-five years old when he died, suggesting this lack of telomerase brought on an earlier than normal death for one so privileged and protected.

The only other possible way for a loss of telomerase so early on in life is because of a major mutation. Since Akhenaten didn't die of old age, so thus having lost most of his telomerase enzyme, this had to be due to a major mutation. Further evidence for this idea comes from the fact that microscopic examination of the DNA showed signs of "nucleotide cicatrix." When found, this is a sure sign DNA has been subjected to powerful mutating agents, or "mutagens."

Therefore, there seems real scientific evidence to suppose this so intelligent pharaoh, who was so far ahead of his time in developing a monotheistic religion, and reviled for having done this, may well have had genetic manipulation performed on him. If not, researchers simply can't account for the strangeness of his genome.

Further evidence of something strange going on with Akhenaten's genome is that his skull, on the nanoscale (extremely small scale) was fundamentally different from that of the skulls of other mummy samples. Akhenaten's skull shows a stronger skull structure than those of "normal" skulls of other pharaoh mummies. This, too, seems odd. Not only did the skull form in a much more elongated way than the average skull, thus increasing brain capacity and possibly intelligence, but the skull itself seems to have been genetically altered to support this increased size.

The repercussions of genetic alterations of ancient rulers by some advanced civilization, whether extraterrestrial or not, implies strong interference in human affairs. The importance of this cannot be minimized. For one thing, what was the purpose of such interference? Furthermore, for how long a time and how often has the human genome been subject to such manipulations? These are answers we need, because if there have been manipulations of our species, we need to know, to know why, and to understand what the consequences of such actions might be for our species.

Do we have other evidence for extraterrestrial interference on Earth? Well, in previous books, I've mentioned the Star Child Skull, found in Mexico and having a makeup very different from standard skulls. The Star Child Skull has had DNA tests done on it. Half the DNA is human and the other half is "unknown." This skull, although not an elongated one, per se, is still a very strange shape.

Elongated skulls for many researchers constitute clear evidence of extraterrestrial visitations in our ancient past, and throughout our history. However, of late, we've come up with even more intriguing evidence of alien interference. Besides, the DNA tests done on the mummy of Akhenaten, we also have this discovery, as reported by Stuart Hooper on February 13, 2015:

9. **Disappearance of Ancient Europeans**. Here is an unusual thing, but one that also seems to show evidence of some type of DNA or genetic tampering with humans. Europeans, according to mainstream researchers in the field, once had dark skins and light eyes. This was at about a mere 7500 to 4500 years ago. We know this because of the unearthing of remains of such people in central Europe, their DNA evidence.

Then, "something strange happened," as one researcher put it. The peoples of central Europe went through a sudden and "radical transformation." Again, this was about 7000 to 4500 years ago. Humans in the area became lighter-skinned and light-eyed. The reason for this is a mystery and researchers of the subject are at a loss to explain this rapid transformation. Because of the time of the occurrence, however, they feel the last glacial period of the Ice Age had little or nothing to do with it. This is because the glaciers were already in deep retreat from the area and had been for several millennia, at least.

Again, scientists are at a loss to explain the cause, for as of this date, no such cause has been found. Nothing seems to indicate why this suddenly took place. However, the time this occurred is coincidental in that it is in the years before the beginning of the rise of modern civilization, having occurred shortly just before or just after this was getting into full swing.

10. Microscopic Space Spheres. At the University of Buckingham, in Great Britain, microscopic "spheres" or "seeds," as some researchers call them, have been discovered. Milton Wainwright, astrobiologist, along with several researchers were studying what they had retrieved by way of a sample-gathering means at high altitude. Although most of the sample contained dust from the high atmosphere, the researchers also found microscopic spheres, and according to them, they are no bigger than a human hair in width.

These spheres contained some sort of material, biological in nature, in a sticky substance. On the exterior of the sphere were filaments, also of a seemingly biological nature. The shell of the sphere was made from metal, a titanium/vanadium alloy, and not of natural origins.

Wainright, along with his fellow researchers, theorize the spheres are alien in nature, not of this world, and are artificial constructs. They think they may be a sort of "space seed," as they put it, intent on seeding other planets in the cosmos with life. Whether this is true or not, is still unknown, but whatever these spherules are, they are not natural in origin. Is this how life began on Earth, through some sort of deliberate panspermia conducted by alien species in other star systems?

Alternatively, is this something else, something darker? A few researchers openly wonder if these metal spheres contain not the beginning of life, but rather something that might alter existing life. They theorize this might be a simple if indirect way of colonizing worlds already sustaining life, with types more suitable to such alien intelligences.

In line with this, I have to mention recent findings about the not-so-common octopus. One scientist actually referred to them as a true "alien life form." This is because, although they contain recognizable genes, the genes of the octopus are distributed in a radically different way than any other known species on Earth. It should also be mentioned that although short-lived, the octopus, and the related species, the squids, are considered very intelligent creatures. The octopus, for example is known for problem solving, as well as using tools. It may be no accident that in many science fiction movies the alien creatures have tentacles. Maybe, we humans realize there is something alien about the octopus on an instinctual, gut level.

Then there is this recent discovery, as well:

11. **FBR (Fast Radio Bursts) of a Mathematical Nature Discovered.** Fast Radio Bursts are not to be confused with perytons, which are much closer to home and probably are the result of energy from nothing more suspicious than microwave ovens. Fast Radio Bursts are very like perytons in some ways, but there are major differences. However, despite this fact, upon discovering that perytons had such a common source as someone probably microwaving their lunch, when FBRs were first discovered many scientists dismissed the discovery for this reason.

However, these mysterious bursts do not seem to be coming from anywhere near Earth at all, and certainly not from microwave ovens. In fact, they don't seem to be emanating even from our galaxy, but rather from some source much farther away. This is because the spread-out nature of the frequencies in these bursts is indicative of the burst having traveled a very long distance.

Therefore, the FBRS must be a result of having traveled extremely long distances, as well, and there is no way they could then be perytons.

In addition, verification that these FBRs were, indeed, from far away came when researchers at the Arecibo Radio Telescope Observatory announced they'd seen a FRB, or Lorimer Burst, as they are also known. These two radio telescopes, spaced thousands of kilometers apart and in difference hemispheres had both managed to spot the same anomaly, and this made for confirmation the FBRs are a real phenomenon.

FBRs last only a few milliseconds, a very short fraction of time, and therefore must have a small, but extremely powerful source to be able to travel so far. Moreover, they seem mathematical in nature, having a definite pattern to them. One of the most troubling problems for astronomers is this anomaly, because it means the FBRs don't conform to what would be expected from known physics.

The stretched-out waves of the frequencies of all the FBRs have helped to show that every burst discovered over the last fifteen years as being in multiples of the number, 1875. The problem is scientists do not have any idea of what could be causing such a bizarre thing, since the FBRs fit no known possible explanation or natural process to cause such a result. Some scientists openly speculate whether the FBRs are the product of intelligence. If so, that intelligence is definitely "out there," being well outside of not only our solar system, but our galaxy, as well.

Furthermore, and this is exciting as it is frightening in a way, *the probability these FBRs, based on this mathematical pattern as just being a natural coincidence, is only five in 10,000!* In other words, one would be better off not betting their farm or house on these being of natural origin! They would almost certainly lose, if they did.

Because of the energy required to broadcast even such a short but powerful burst on all frequencies, scientists say it would require extraterrestrials of a Type II civilization on the Kardashev Scale. By comparison, humans have yet to achieve even a Type I civilization. This means we would be dealing with a civilization so advanced that we would appear as worse than primitive apes to them.

What does all this mean? Well, either we need to develop a newer model of physics to incorporate FBRs into the world of natural phenomenon, or as one of Fred Hoyle's characters in one of his science fiction novels, *The Black Cloud*, rather profanely put it: *"There are bastards out there."* meaning aliens do exist in deep space.

The purpose of the FBRs is not clear as to what they might actually mean, but that they exist, are real anomalies, now is beyond doubt. Just what they are, why they exist remains an incredible enigma. However, the implications if they are artificial in origin are immense, indeed!

12. NASA Predicts Discovery of Alien Life. As a final note on this subject as to whether or not extraterrestrials existed or even can exist, it should also be mentioned that just recently, NASA announced it fully expects to find evidence for alien life by 2025, if not before. This is predicted by none other than NASA's Chief Scientist. She said:

"I think we're going to have strong indications of life beyond Earth within a decade, and I think we're going to have definitive evidence within twenty to thirty years."

Again, this was according to NASA Chief Scientist, Ellen Stofan, and it was her statement in April of 2015.

But what does this mean for our puzzle of what happened here on Earth around 12,000 or more years ago? Well, for one thing, there seems to be a lot of evidence of late pointing to the fact that alien life, and very likely, intelligent alien life does exist. Then if it exists now "out there," it must have also existed long ago. For instance, if the FRB turn out to be some sort of sign of intelligent life of a Type II alien civilization, then we are talking about one very likely to be millions of light years away. After all, our nearest galaxy is Andromeda, and that's 2.537 million light years away. If they are this far away, then that means the FBRs are millions of years old. So intelligent life could well have been around in the universe for a very long time.

Another factor also suggests this; recently, cosmologists have determined that rocky worlds, such as our Earth, may have started forming much earlier on in the history of the universe than originally thought. This means life and intelligent life could have started on them much longer ago than was believed possible up until now.

Yes, life is quite probably "out there," and even more importantly, it may well have come to Earth in our past, and perhaps more than once, and by more than one species. Do we have any evidence for this also being true? Once more, it seems we do, and we will discuss it in the next chapter.

CHAPTER 14

ALIENS ON EARTH

Could aliens have really existed on Earth? If so, they would form another important piece of our puzzle, perhaps the most important piece of all, since it would explain many things about our past. Amazingly, there is evidence for someone having visited here and from a variety of sources over long periods. We have not only written records of such events, but we have archaeological evidence, as well

Remember those ooparts, a few of which were mentioned earlier on? Well, there are a lot more than just those, literally thousands of them. I don't want to recite all of those I mention in my book *Megalithia, Ancient Alien Empire*, but there are a few outstanding ones that really do have to be considered here again, as well.

1. **The Dashka Stone or "The Map of the Creator."** Russian scientists have done further testing on the Dashka Stone and have found it to be about 120 million years old. Made of three layers of different types of minerals, which these same scientists say couldn't have occurred naturally together this way, with a form of see-through "glaze" as the top layer. The map, found in the region, shows an area in the Ural Mountains

complete with river systems and no less than twelve dams that don't exist today, but are engraved on the stone. Part of what must have been a much larger map, for legends in the area speak of as many as twenty such stones, the Dashka Stone is 1.524 meters high by 1.06 meters wide. Therefore, the original stone map must have been gigantic in size.

The weirdest thing of all about the map is that it shows the region as if from a great height, and with a definite three-dimensional quality. The map looks to be the results of either a high altitude survey of the region, or even from some orbiting device. If this is so, then modern humans didn't make this map, at least not without help, for it was far before we had such capabilities.

The Russian scientists, a team of them, are adamant about their findings, saying they have tested and retested the stone. The stone is mentioned here, because despite a battery of more recent tests, the Dashka Stone still defies the odds and seems to be truly an ancient work by "someone." The carving is estimated to be thousands (25,000 years or more according to some estimates) of years old, although the stone they are engraved on is far older, by millions of years.

There is an interesting addition to the whole question of the Dashka Stone—there is writing on it, a form of hieroglyphics that were originally thought to be a form of ancient Chinese, but have since been determined not to be. The writing bears a marked resemblance to the hieroglyphics/writing on objects found elsewhere in the world, such as the World Map Stone in South America.

So what do we have here, exactly? Well, to sum it up, we have a part of a truly huge stone map, one compounded of three different layers of stone. The map depicts an entire region, complete with major dams and earthworks and diversions of a river, no less, and all in a three-dimensional format. Finally, the age of the map, although in dispute because of the uncertainties of dating it, is said to date back at least 25,000 years, and this is no hoax! Moreover, rumors about missing portions of the map have circulated for at least a century or more.

What does this mean for our timeline? Well, someone did all this, the map, and more, and if it wasn't us, then it had to be someone from "out there." Only someone with an amazingly advanced technology could have undertaken such huge tasks as altering river courses in the Ural Mountains, placing dams and creating lakes where for water supplies where there had been none, creating irrigation systems, as well.

Furthermore, it is important to remember here that the Pre-Adamites had a penchant for building things to last. This seems to be one of their hallmarks of their civilization. However, although dams can exist for thousands of years, they are, ultimately, temporary structures. Water will have its way and nothing lasts forever. When the dams ultimately failed, for whatever reason, whether due to their maintenance having been abandoned by the Pre-Adamites, or the Pre-Adamites having abandoned the region entirely, the result would have been the same. The dams would have failed and the rivers would have reverted to their old courses.

2. **Twenty Thousand Year-Old Spiral "Screws."** Also found in the Ural Mountains of Russia was thousands of spiral shaped metal objects, described as "screws" for want of a better description. First discovered by gold prospectors along a stream and adjacent river in the early 1990s, these objects vary in size, but none of them is large. The largest is no more than 3.15 centimeters in length, with the smallest being as little as 0.000254 centimeters in size, truly a nanoscale object. Moreover, although some of these objects were found on the surface, most have been discovered at a depth of from anywhere from three to twelve meters deep in the ground.

Again, they were found in several locations along the Narada, Balbanyu, and the Koszhim Rivers, as well as along two nearby streams. This strongly implies that at some time in the distant past, they washed down the streams and rivers from somewhere upstream. Then deposits of silt buried them. Judging by the depth they were buried, this has to have been a very long time ago, thousands upon thousands of years. Moreover, there are thousands of these "screws" discovered and still more are coming to light.

Made of various materials, the screws are composed of alloys including tungsten and the much rarer molybdenum for the tiniest, with the larger ones being composed of copper. The problem with this find is the type of metals used for the smallest "screws." These can only be refined at astonishingly high temperatures, with tungsten having a melting point of 6100 degrees Fahrenheit, and molybdenum requiring no less than 4740 degrees to melt. To date, testing the age of the "screws" consistently shows them to be approximately 20,000 years in age.

What does this mean? Well, someone was doing extremely advanced metallurgy and on the nanoscale 20,000 years ago, long before humans were supposed to have any real type of metallurgical skills at all, let alone the ability to create so many objects on so tiny a scale.

Likewise, what use would truly primitive humans have for such things? What function would they fulfill? No, someone else had to be creating and using such "screws," and since they weren't humans, they had to be "someone" else. In addition, the age and location of the finds puts them close to the region depicted as if from the air on the Dashka Stone. This would hardly seem to be just a coincidence.

3. **Geode with "Spark Plug" Inside, 1961.** In California, a geode was found in the Coso Mountains. When opened, the stone contained, embedded inside, a distinctly artificial looking object. X-rays were taken. The object had a material that seemed to be ceramic in nature. Inside of this was a metal "core." A wooden exterior surrounded all of this. The object looked very similar to a spark plug, no less, but probably was some type of electric part that only bore a resemblance to such an object. The geode, covered with a layer of fossils and completely sealed when found, is approximately 500,000 years in age. This puts it well back past the time of even the Dashka Stone.

The true purpose of the thing, whatever it is, is unknown. The fact it must be close to 500,000 years old is intriguing. Were primitive humans driving around Fords and Chevrolets with such "spark plugs?" Not hardly. So again, we have "someone" else who must have created and used this oopart, for some unknown purpose.

4. **Ancient "Tracks" Found in Turkey and Malta.** Now this is a truly controversial subject and a very strange one. An actual geologist makes the claim that there are tracks of some kind of vehicles to be found in Turkey. These tracks, he says, were laid down by some "unknown and intelligent" race or species some 12 million years ago or perhaps even longer. Dr. Alexander Koltypin of the Natural Science Scientific Research Center in Russia says there are a series of tracks, which he claims, are "petrified tracking ruts." These are embedded in solidified volcanic ash, which makes the age of the tracks datable.

Dr. Koltypin further says the tracks are the result of some type of vehicles that made a habit of traveling back and forth across the then soft rock, which being composed of such a malleable material, wore under the constant wear and tear of such vehicles passing over it. This occurred in the area of Phrygia, and this route was used by many civilizations that rose and fell over time, including, but not limited to, the Hittites, Greeks, Macedonians, and Romans. Some of the tracks even became part of the later Roman road network that tied that mighty empire together.

Nor is this area the only place such types of ruts exist. Malta is repeatedly crisscrossed with similar ancient tracks and many of these go right down into the sea, showing they existed well before the rise of the oceans with the melting of the last glacial period of the Ice Age.

Dr. Koltypin insists it is very likely that these are actual tracks of vehicles of some sort, and furthermore, they were not, at least not originally, the result of carts, chariots, or such later primitive human vehicles. He claims this because:

a. The tracks are far too old to be these, and...

b. The ruts are too deep, meaning the vehicles were of a much heavier type to cause such wear into the soft stone over time. In fact, he states the ruts could well be the result of "unknown antediluvian all-terrain vehicles," since the wheelbase is different from that of our cars and chariots of ancient times. They are much closer in width to our modern automobiles.

Once again, we have this reference to something truly prehistoric and "antediluvian" in nature. Dr. Koltypin specifically argues that humans, because of the ruts' extreme age, could not have made the tracks. Furthermore, they aren't just any sort of geological accident, since there are far too many over a wide area of rocky fields. Some of the ruts actually show curves to them and cross over older tracks, as if routes changed slightly over time. He claims this is clearly the case, since there is extensive erosion of the stone tracks, which shows their age.

Nor are these minor ruts. Some are up to a meter in depth! Also, rather than just being meandering ruts that run somewhat parallel to each other, they are at precise distances from each other, and this distance does not vary at all. They maintain the same width from each other throughout their entire length. If they were natural products of some strange type of erosion, this shouldn't be possible.

In addition, there are what Dr. Koltypin describes as regular scratches along the inside edges of the ruts, as of some sort of spoke system having rubbed along them, or some type of axles. He says the deepness of the ruts was a direct result of the heavy nature of the vehicles involved. The prehistoric mysterious vehicle tracks, as found in the Phrygian Valley of Turkey, were similar i scale to those a modern car would make.

Like so many frustrated mainstream scientists who arrive at conclusions based on the evidence, which appears contradictory to what the majority of scientists want to believe, Dr. Koltypin knows he is fighting an uphill battle with his claims. He says he faces such opposition because it casts into doubt everything most scientists currently believe about the history of intelligent life on Earth. Dr. Koltypin further bolsters his claim by the many ruts found on the Island of Malta, which for him constitutes proof this wasn't some one-off weird type of natural but unexplained phenomenon. He cites the fact that such ruts exist all over the Maltese archipelago, including at Misrah Ghar il-Kbir, as proof of this.

I have seen the tracks in Malta and they are impressive. Nobody seems to know who made them, but that they were made long ago isn't in doubt. The tracks, in many cases, are worn right through hard stone. One even goes right over a cliff, while as I mentioned earlier, others just go down and into the sea. They crisscross each other and run everywhere. There is just no way they can be of natural origin. In short, the tracks in Malta, as well as those in Turkey are a complete and compelling mystery.

Now, I could go on here cataloguing countless ooparts. Everything from 50,000 year-old abandoned mines in Utah, so old the exposed coal is completely oxidized, to a hand bell found inside a solid lump of coal, and much, much more. However, my purpose here isn't to do an endless recitation of such facts, but rather to try to piece a great puzzle together. For this reason, due to limited space, I include a few of the more interesting and most recent discoveries, rather than resorting to a lengthy catalogue of them. Still, for those who wish more of this please, see the links I've provided to such topics listed under "References" at the end of this book.

The number, types, and descriptions of such things are truly fascinating, though. Even more fascinating is why anyone as far back as the 1700s, or 1800s would attempt to create so many hoaxes. This seems unlikely. Moreover, as with the "screws," there simply isn't really a means for them having done so. Nor is there any rational purpose, it seems.

Again, with regard to the screws, there seems no conceivable way anyone could have buried so many, so perfectly, as not to seem to have disturbed the earth, in so great a region. The effort and time involved to bury them, let alone somehow make all of them, just isn't realistic.

In any case, now that we have seen examples of physical evidence for an ancient and apparently very advanced culture, even more advanced than our civilization today in many ways; do we also have any written texts from our recorded history, which might also serve to bolster our case? Again, we do, and they come from various cultures around the world. Still, one of the most complete examples of references to otherworldly beings come from the Hindu vedic texts of India.

5. **Rigveda.** Many of us know about the *Ramayana* and the *Mahabharata* texts, if only from various ancient aliens shows on television, and once more, I've spoken of these in my other books, as well, but there is another one that talks of alien races, and this is the *Rigveda*.

The *Rigveda* is perhaps one of the oldest texts, if not the oldest one, in the world, since it does not mention the other *Vedas*. This logically implies it had to have been written first, since the other texts do mention it, in return and so must have come later. There are thousands of lines of text in the Rigveda, but some lines from it are of particular significance for us here.

These lines of the text not only refer to the "Generation of the Gods," but talk about the beginning of the universe, itself, along with a number of stars (seven) in particular, the ones referred to as the "Adityas." The Rigveda text goes on to say these stars were created before the gods, themselves. The text also states that eventually the gods found another star, which as it turns out, was our Sun. The text mentions there was a world with life on it there, similar to theirs, and meaning Earth, it would seem, and us.

There is more. The texts make many references, but the sum of it all is that:

a. The texts say the universe was created first, undergoing something very like our cosmological concept of a Big Bang.

b. The gods were a later creation, which makes logical sense, and were perfectly aware of how the universe began, understood the concept of the Big Bang.

c. The gods eventually happened upon our solar system.

d. This is a very important point; the gods (aliens?) were involved in a deadly war with those referred to as the Asuras. Again, this last is important, for according to the Rigveda and the other Vedic texts on this subject, this war came to our world, and our Moon might very well have been the thing that brought it here, or at least played a telling part in events, as we shall see later on.

6. Mahabharata. We can't move on without mentioning the Mahabharata, another Hindu text, as well, since it so explicitly talks about a great war played out on the land and in the air above India. This text specifically talks about the destruction of major cities of the Rama Empire, as well as entire armies, by using flying devices referred to in the texts as "vimanas." These airborne vehicles came in various sizes, some as large as fortresses, and others much smaller. Here is one direct example from the text itself:

"Gurkha, flying a swift and powerful vimanas hurled a single projectile (rocket) charged with the power of the Universe. An incandescent column of smoke and flame, as bright as ten thousand suns, rose with all its splendor. It was an unknown weapon, an iron thunderbolt, a gigantic messenger of death, which reduced to ashes the entire race of the Vrishnis and the Andhakas.

We need to focus on one particular phrase of that quotation, *"charged with the power of the Universe."* This is highly significant, because all suns in the universe derive their energy from fusion reactions taking place deep within them, by converting hydrogen to helium. Moreover, this is exactly how the hydrogen bomb works, by fusion, thus utilizing the same principles as suns. And the phrase "iron thunderbolt" sounds very much like a missile.

Is it no wonder then, that Robert Oppenheimer, the so-called "Father of the Atomic Bomb" quoted Hindu texts regarding Shiva, the Destroyer, when our first nuclear bomb was tested (fission bomb, not fusion). The comparison to this text above is apt, and seems to show that if not a nuclear device used to destroy these Rama Empire cities, than something so similar as to be hard to tell the difference was!

The aftermath, too, sounds incredibly like what one would find after a nuclear explosion:

"The corpses were so burned as to be unrecognizable. Hair and nails fell out. Pottery broke without apparent cause, and the birds turned white. After a few hours all foodstuffs were infected... to escape from this fire the soldiers threw themselves in streams to wash themselves and their equipment."

Here, we have remarkable descriptions so similar to what occurs after a nuclear blast, with regard to radioactive fallout, that one would be hard pressed to write a more accurate version today.

Again, I don't want to belabor the point here about the vedic texts, because many others have mentioned these points before. However, they had to be included, at least to some extent here, because they are just such compelling pieces of evidence, or recorded information of a great war, one that seems to have gone nuclear.

The texts also talk of a time when there was a great war going on, one between the gods and the demons. There are also compelling sections that refer to things very much like rockets, as here in the *Mahabharata*:

"...At Rama`s behest, the magnificent chariot rose up to a mountain of cloud with a tremendous din."

And another reference:

"...Bhima flew with his Vimana on an enormous ray which was as brilliant as the sun and made a noise like the thunder of a storm."

If some think this does not describe interplanetary travel necessarily, there is this quotation from the Vymanka-Shastra:

"An apparatus which can go by its own force, from one place to place or globe to globe."

"Globe to globe is a pretty clear indication these vimanas had the capability of traveling to other planets. As Dr. Raghavan, an expert on the subject says, no less than thirty-one separate parts are described in the texts, and that no less than sixteen kinds of metal were used in the construction of the vimanas.

These vimanas, as another expert on the subject of the texts points out, Dr. A.V. Krishan Murty, a Professor of Aeronautics, were vessels whose design was based on "spaceships coming from other planets." An incredible statement and one that clearly shows the relationship of the vimanas to other types of alien craft, since the design of the vimanas was, according to the professor, predicated on them. Convincing, stuff, really, coming from experts, as it does.

The texts also refer to humans piloting some of the craft as special servants to the "gods." The pilots were the elite, special, and underwent extensive training. Moreover, the texts describe some of what they had to learn, such as how to avoid midair collisions, for instance, how to fly from place to place, etc. Again, incredible stuff, considering these texts are supposedly just the stuff of legend, if one believes western sources.

Nor is the ancient Indian culture alone is asserting such a thing as flying vessels. The *Hakatha*, or the *Laws of the Babylonians*, says much the same thing, when it asserts that flying such vessels was a privilege, a special reward from "those from upon high." In this case, it would seem "those" were quite literally from "on high" in the literal sense, being from outer space.

Apparently, the privilege of being allowed to fly such craft was bestowed upon humans to help them move about more freely and much more quickly, to aid others and perhaps even save lives. This is rather reminiscent of medical/hospital helicopters, which do the same thing today. Additionally, only the most favored, the most trusted, and the most proficient at flying such vessels were allowed to use them.

The vedic texts go on at very considerable length on the subject of the Great War fought among the gods, as well as on Earth, and the amount of description and material is impressive. The vimanas varied in size and purpose, with some being as large as "cities," while others were much smaller. The Vedic texts mention that there were approximately 400 different races involved in this ancient war and that many, if not most, were not human. The term "demons" is often used to describe them.

7. **Ancient Chaldeans.** The Chaldeans were a Semitic people who existed around the time of 1000 BCE. In the *Sifrala*, a Chaldean work, there are the equivalent to about one hundred pages of what can only be described as in-depth or technical data on how to build a flying machine. The information sounds very modern when translated, because it includes references to such things as graphite rods, copper coils, and much more.

   Again, we have another and independent historical record, an incredibly detailed one about such flying machines, and even how they were built, as if someone were attempting to preserve such knowledge for the ages. This, despite the fact they may well not have had the capability of creating such aircraft themselves. Rather they were simply recording what they knew about those who did build them, their methods and materials. These references are from D. Hatcher Childress, who wrote a very complete compendium on the subject of such ancient Flying Machines. (See "References," at end of this book for links to his work.)

8. **Mohenjo-Daro.** Then there are the physical ruins as evidence, such as the ancient city of Mohenjo-Daro. This metropolis city had stood for a long time and deep in the layers of earth beneath it, earlier ruins of the city show a time when the metropolis was struck by an intense fire, one so heated that people dropped as they ran. This was supposed to have been in the time of that "mythical" Rama Empire, as the vedic texts describe things.

   What's more, there is strong evidence for vitrification of pottery shards at this layer of the archaeological digs, and evidence for city having been flash-burned. Vitrification is the process whereby earthenware objects, sand, and other natural materials composed of stone transmute into a type of glass, "vitrified glass."

The first that modern civilization really became aware of such a phenomenon was after the first nuclear detonations in White Sands, New Mexico. Examination of the blast site afterwards showed such vitrification having taken place. What's more, only extreme heat, of the thermonuclear kind, a lightning strike in some instances, erupting volcano, or that of an impacting asteroid could cause such vitrification. Again, to vitrify pottery, to turn clay into a glass, requires tremendous heat.

There is no sign there were ever any volcanoes in the area of Mohenjo-Daro. There is no sign of an asteroid impact, no shocked quartz crystal to provide such a clue, not a crater, etc. Lightning could hardly have caused such vitrification on so large a scale over so wide an area.

The only thing left, by the sheer process of elimination, seems to be a thermonuclear blast. What's more, some of the skeletons at the site had a radiation level much higher than the surrounding natural background radiation of the area. Also, some stone walls (one side of them only, as if from a tremendous flash of heat), show vitrification, as well, and this runs in a ring around a central area, as if the perimeter of a blast site.

Furthermore, this isn't the only site to show such vitrification. The ruins of truly ancient forts in Scotland, Ireland, as well as Germany, also show signs of this, as well. The stone of which these structures had been made shows definite signs of this, yet the same stone material in the countryside not far from the ruins (undoubtedly where the stone for the structures was originally obtained) show no sign of having undergone such a vitrification process. Something incredibly hot struck at that stone to cause it to become glass-like, and whatever it was, happened a long time ago. We have no way of knowing for sure just how long, because once more, we can't date a stone structure as to when it was constructed.

Do we have more sources of information about a great war amongst aliens, one that also involved us humans? Yes we do. Not discounting the Bible and its references to a major war in the heavens between God, his angels, and the "Fallen," we do have a number of other sources for such a thing having really taken place. Practically every civilization on Earth has some sort of ancient legends and/or myths, which refer to such an event having occurred.

9. **Götterdämmerung.** This, as mentioned earlier in passing, is a legend of the Norsemen, with their gods having been involved in a great battle, literally one named the Dusk of the Gods, "Götterdämmerung," because it was their downfall. This battle was on a tremendous scale, took place everywhere, including in the heavens, and resulted in the final defeat of the Norse gods. They fought the good fight, it seems, but still lost.

10. **The Titans and the Olympians.** Many people are aware of this legend, thanks to modern movies on the subject of a colossal war between the gods of old, the Titans, and the gods of Mt. Olympus, the "Olympians." The war, again a battle in the heavens and elsewhere, was a "titanic" one (the word "titanic" being derived from "Titan"), and resulted in the downfall of those ancient and so-powerful beings.

11. **Native Americans.** Whether one looks at North, Central, or South America, native tribes of various regions have their tales of great wars having been fought amongst their gods with attendant mass destruction. Although the stories often differ greatly in details, the central theme is the same: great battles among powerful beings were fought, often in the skies or on mountaintops, it seems. Moreover, there was always a "good versus evil" quality to these tales.

12. **China.** China had its Dragon Gods, who fought great battles in the sky, among other places and which could breathe fire, if they chose. The Chinese, too, had their heaven, "Tian." Even the first Emperor of China was supposed to have come to Earth on a "fiery dragon." Many researchers, ancient alien theorists, think these references to fiery dragons were actually references to spacecraft of some type or other. So, was the First Emperor of China an alien, a Nephilim or Watcher?

Cultures all over the Earth have myths of ancient and powerful beings that controlled our world, and who then ended up doing great battles, underwent a great war of some sort. In many cases, the legends describe these gods as losing the battle and thus disappearing from our world.

This is a rather bizarre thing. Usually, if one is telling a story to show the moral implications of good versus evil, then "good" should triumph. In many cases with such tales, though, this isn't so, and more often than not. Revered gods of many cultures seem instead to have lost their battles and their control of the peoples they "governed." This would seem counterproductive to such tales, for it shows "evil" triumphing rather than good.

Mind you, many of these legends also describe those gods who ruled humanity as being vain, capricious, and destructive, using humans as their playthings more often than not. Although, there always seems to be some gods who are sympathetic to humanity, as with the Titan god, Prometheus, who tried to help humans by giving them fire, only to suffer disastrous consequences for doing so. The other gods, it seemed, did not want humans to have any sort of knowledge or abilities, especially those they reserved for themselves.

This punishing those who tried to obtain knowledge holds true even for the Bible. Quite clearly, the "forbidden" tree in the story of Adam and Eve is the Tree of Knowledge, and not the Tree of Life. Knowledge was the only "forbidden fruit." The fallen angel, Lucifer, whose name in one version of the translation means "light," was punished for eternity for daring to give Adam and Eve knowledge.

This is a theme in so many cultures around the world, the punishing of those who give humans knowledge, that one can't help but wonder why this is so. The gods did not want humans to have knowledge, not of any sort. Even when allowed to serve them as pilots for their flying machines, it was only the select and privileged few allowed to do so. To serve the gods, it seems, was an honor and something to be desired, even if it was hard work.

If the gods were in reality extraterrestrials, it seems they were few in numbers and so needed our help, however, that help was foisted upon us as a thing of great honor and privilege, and was restricted to only the most trustworthy humans. Not an uncommon approach for masters who are distrustful of their slaves, as history all too often has shown us repeatedly.

PART FOUR

THE ENDING

CHAPTER 15

THE GREAT FLOOD

As I'm sure many readers by now may have noticed, we had been moving slowly backwards in time. We started at the current era, and then moved back to the rise of modern civilization, 3500 BCE. After that, we entered what I refer to as the so-called Stagnant Period of humanity. This was the 6500 years of time prior to the rise of civilization. This in turn, finally brings us back to the time of 10,000 BCE, about 12,000 years ago.

We have also talked about various pieces of our timeline puzzle. Many of them fall into this last period, the Stagnant Period of humanity, or even further back in time, predating 10,000 BCE by thousands, or some cases, even millions of years, That is, if one accepts the validity of at least some of the ooparts embedded in coal and rock. However, for now, let's focus on 10,000 BCE, or 12,000 years ago. Something momentous occurred at this time. By this, the reference is to the Great Flood, of course, the same flood as of Noah's Ark fame.

Scientists have uncovered one region where a "Great Flood" did occur. This was the Black Sea, which as previously mentioned, was once a large freshwater lake, but then, over a short space of time, in-filled with seawater from the rising Mediterranean Sea.

This has some written historical backing. Ancient records describe such an event as having occurred during the time of some Greek kings, one of whom, the Dardanelle Straits was later named after. Underwater ruins, some at a depth of no less than 100 meters, show there were occupied areas at one time. This was where, according to archaeologists and geologists, the old original shoreline was, when the Black Sea was still a freshwater lake. The in-filling took place very quickly; geologically speaking it was in the blink of an eye. Estimates are it took only thirty years for this flooding to happen. In fact, so quickly did this occur that original dunes along the old shoreline weren't even eroded away, but rather were just submerged. This is a sure sign of a rapid flooding of the area, because tidal action didn't have a chance to wash the dunes away.

When exactly did this happen? Well, as mentioned, we have the records of such a flood occurring in ancient Greek times, but other researchers argue it happened much earlier, even as long as 6000 years ago, which puts it well before the time of the Greek kings by thousands of years. Scientists rely on the Carbon-14 method of dating to determine the age of the event, but this method is unreliable when dating saltwater marine deposits. The results can be very skewed at times. Such researchers think that perhaps a later and final flooding occurred, of which the written records then speak of, but the first flooding of the Black Sea came much earlier.

In any case, given this new evidence, again, scientists say they may have accounted for the origin of the myths of a Great Flood. However, based on the evidence available, it is other researchers' contention the Great Flood was not a flood restricted just to the Mediterranean/Middle Eastern region of Europe and Asia.

There was more than the Black Sea and just the surrounding area involved, it seems clear. Rather, there is much evidence to support the idea that the deluge was, instead, a worldwide event. The Great Flood then, was a global phenomenon and not just a regional one. Of course, to dare make such a statement, one had better be able to produce evidence of such a theory. Here are some good examples that support the idea the Great Flood was more than just a regional event. One of the most obvious points is that flood legends are:

1. From around the world, and not just the Mediterranean region, and...

2. They usually talk of some person (man) who saved the people by building an ark, boat, raft, or the like. If the Black Sea took approximately thirty years to fill, there would be no reason for this. One could simply walk away, at a snail's pace if one chose, from any waters rising so comparatively slowly. Still, even without using this logic, we have a lot more to go on.

3. **Sumeria.** The famous Sumerian *List of Kings* divides into two main sections, those that ruled Sumeria before the Flood, and those who ruled after. Those rulers who existed before the deluge were, according to the list itself, said to be possessed of very long lifespans, measured in hundreds or thousands of years.

After the deluge, the lifespans altered, became the human norm. The time of the Flood, itself, seems to have been the dividing line. The Sumerian story of the Great Flood was discovered on the *Deluge Tablet*. This was from the Ziusudra Epic, and spoke of a "Divine Counsel." Ziusudra was the Sumerian equivalent to Noah, and he built a ship, as Noah did the Ark, in order to survive the deluge. Although ancient Sumeria is near the Black Sea, they weren't on it, per se, and the Black Sea rise should hardly have affected the majority of Sumerians who lived far enough away from the region at the time.

4. **Babylon.** The Babylonians, too, had their account of the deluge. Although there were a number of versions of the Great Flood with them, they follow pretty much the same idea. In the written 700 BCE version, in the *Epic of Gilgamesh*, he, Gilgamesh, meets a god ("immortal"). The immortal's name is Utnapishtim. Utnapishtim, favored by the god Ea, built a ship

so that he and his family could survive the Great Flood. This is close to the biblical version found in Genesis 6-9. Again, like Noah, who was blessed with the ability to live to an extreme age, so is Utnapishtim likewise blessed by the gods and is considered immortal for all practical purposes.

5. **Hebrew Bible.** The Hebrew Bible says much the same, with the God, Yahweh, telling Noah to build an ark to save himself and his family. He also tells him to save animals, as well. Whether this was all animals, or just domesticated livestock necessary for Noah and his family's survival, is a point of contention among theologians. In addition, many theologians and historians say the Jews may have absorbed some of the so-called mythology of the Babylonians, who in turn had absorbed it from the more ancient Sumerians.

This is certainly possible. The Babylonians held the Jews for a while in captivity. Still, this does not explain the fact this same "legend" is worldwide in nature. Did the Sumerians also hand it down to Native Americans of North and South America, as well as Asia, and elsewhere? This would hardly seem likely.

6. **Plato's *Timaeus*.** In his work, the *Dialogue of Timaeus*, Plato not only speaks of Atlantis, but he also talks of a race of "Bronze Humans," who, because they dared make war on Zeus, were to face the devastation of a Great Flood. However, one of the Titans, again Prometheus, instructed Deucalion to build a ship and so save himself and his family. As with so many other versions of this flood tale, the ship or ark came to rest after nine days on a mountain, in this case, Mount Parnassus.

7. **Hindu Satapatha Brahmana Texts**. In these religious Hindu texts there is the story of the Great Flood being told, as well. The texts say that Matsay, the Avatar of Vishnu of the times, warned Manu of a deluge to come. Again, we have a deity or demigod who instructs a human to build a great ship to save

himself and those he loves. In this case, India is far removed from the region of the Middle East. Yet, this story of a Great Flood is intrinsic in the ancient works of the Indian Hindu culture, as well.

8. **Australian Aboriginal Tale of the Dreamtime**. In one of the native peoples of Australia Dreamtime tales is the story of the frog, Tiddalik. He first drinks up all the water on Earth, but then, through the manipulation of other animals, releases it in one vast flood that replenishes all the lakes, streams, rivers, etc., but causes a real problem for the natives of Australia.

9. **Native North American Tales. Nanabozho (Various Spellings) and the Great Serpent**. In this tale, we hear the story of a young warrior who confronts the Great Serpent. The end result is that the Great Serpent, angered, rises from the bottom of a lake and floods all the Earth. The native people had to flee far, to high mountains, as the land and even the hills below them all flooded. Again, we have people in retreat to mountaintops, just the same as we do in Europe, the East, and Far East.

10. **The Cree.** Cree tales speak of a Great Flood.

11. **Arapahos.** The Arapaho have tales of the Great Flood, as well.

12. **Tales From Around the World of the Great Flood.** The stories of there having once been a Great Flood are not only endemic to regions around the world, but seem systemic to them, as well. Always, they are one of the oldest stories told, and always, despite cultural variations, they speak of a Great Flood from which people had to flee in order to save their lives. Whether the Cheyenne, the Seminoles, or whomever, there are tales of the local natives in North America of the Great Flood. This is true even of the Inuit in Northern Canada, as well as natives of South America, and elsewhere. The Great Flood is truly a worldwide legend and not just restricted to one region of the Mediterranean.

ROB SHELSKY

13. Scientific Evidence For A Great Flood—Melting of Glaciers Causes Flood Stories? Scientists say the melting of the last glacial period and the resulting rise in sea levels may have been responsible, or at least contributed to, the Great Flood stories from around the world. This may be closer to the truth than trying to make the in filling of the Black Sea responsible for such global stories.

Unlike many scientists, who see the rising sea levels as a gradual process, others say there is evidence to support the idea it happened much more quickly than thought. At least, some phase or phases of it may have happened swiftly. From the evidence available, it would appear the worst flooding, the most immediate and devastating part of it, probably happened right near the very beginning of the melting of the glaciers, with perhaps lesser, periodic episodes then ensuing over time, mixed with a continual rising of the seas. We will get to more on that later on.

Still, please note that vast areas of land did eventually submerge. Ireland, Britain, Denmark, and France were all once, one continuous land mass. We know this, because extensive settlements have been found at the bottom of the North Sea, which shows the area was once dry land. This tells us that truly great regions became submerged. The maps of the world were very different before the flooding than they appear now.

CHAPTER 16

EVIDENCE FOR "THE GREAT WAR"

So exactly what did happen 12,000 years ago? What caused the glaciers to melt so rapidly? Was whatever occurred, a natural phenomenon or something else? It is the contention of this book, based on the available evidence that something of a truly catastrophic nature occurred around that time. Science has found some real, hard evidence for such an event, but the exact nature of it is still a matter of conjecture for them. They cite multiple possibilities as the cause, but are sure of none of these.

For such a disastrous event to affect the whole planet, then it, of course, would have to have been worldwide in nature. Moreover, it could well have, and I believe it did, result in the Great Flood.

The Process Of Elimination. What type of events worldwide is there that could have such an effect? What could have caused the Great Flood? Well, a large asteroid impact is one possibility. A major and heavy meteorite bombardment would be another. A super volcano erupting might just manage to do the job, although there are problems with this last idea. The super volcano shouldn't have caused the melting of the great glaciers, but rather would probably have initiated another "nuclear-winter" period, where due to the dust in the upper atmosphere thrown there by the super volcano, sunlight would have been severely reduced. The world would have chilled, not warmed. We know this happens, because we have recent historical evidence from the eruptions of several regular volcanoes that this is so.

A cosmic ray burst from space is another possibility. This is a result of the collapse of a star in a supernova or hypernova most often, and can result in a powerful beam of cosmic rays generated. If the Earth happened to be in the way of such a powerful beam, even though light-years distant from the explosion, this could still result in a cataclysmic die-off. Many paleontologists think this may have happened in the far past, and could account for a near extinction-level event for life on our planet, at least one of them.

However, this last has problems, as well. Although a cosmic ray burst might wipe out a lot of life on the planet, it shouldn't have devastated it geologically. Therefore, a cosmic ray burst couldn't account for that.

Furthermore, if there had been a large asteroid impact, we should have remnants of such a crater, as we do in the Yucatán Peninsula for the sixty-five million-year-old asteroid impact there, sounding the death knell of the dinosaurs in the process. Even after sixty-five million years, we can clearly see evidence for such a crater. We also have that distinctive geological marker we spoke of, the boundary line of iridium, as well. Today, we have no evidence for such a type of event occurring in 10,000 BCE. As near as science can tell, an asteroid impact did not occur at that time, at least not one large enough to be the cause of such an event.

So, have we exhausted all natural possibilities as to the probable cause of such a major catastrophe so long ago? Well, there is one more I can think of and that is war, if one wants to consider such a thing natural. This would have to have been a different type of war than we are used to, I freely acknowledge. Moreover, it would require something else, as well, which we will discuss in a later chapter in more detail.

For the moment, let's simply go over the evidence for such a catastrophe, something large enough in scale that it might have triggered the collapse of the continental glaciers, and their melting. There is also evidence that this war might have been very much in the vein of a cold war for a long period, according to the Hindu vedic texts, but then ultimately it flared into full force. Something had to have triggered this last. Was it the arrival of our Moon in orbit around Earth?

As always, we should try to draw evidence from at least several sources to attempt to bolster our theories. So let's have a look at the evidence. We will discuss this in the next chapter.

CHAPTER 17

THE INVADER MOON

Now we come to the chapter that mirrors the title of this book, Invader Moon. Just what do I mean by using this term? Well, rather than trying to explain, let's look at some information first:

Our moon is a very strange satellite. It differs markedly in many ways from any other moon of the solar system. Some brief facts about our moon:

1. The Moon is the largest moon of any rocky world in our solar system.

2. The Moon's density seems to be too low for its size.

3. The Moon has an orbit that is very close to being perfectly circular, when it should definitely be more of an ellipse.

4. The top three layers of the Moon seem "reversed," with the densest material on the surface and lighter layers below it.

5. Only the near side of the Moon has "mares" those huge flat areas that look so dark, that ancient astronomers thought they were seas and so they called them "mares," Latin for "seas."

The far side of the Moon has none of these. What it does have is an abundance of craters. It's covered with them!

6. The origin of the Moon is an ongoing and baffling mystery. Scientists simply can't account for how it came into our skies. There are no fewer than five different main theories as to how this could have happened. All of them seem to have major flaws. In fact, so much so, one of the very latest theories, a newer one, now challenges the impact theory. The impact theory states that a Mars-like object struck the Earth at an angle. This event resulted in a tremendous collision and debris exploded up from the Earth in great quantities. This free-floating debris coalesced into the moon of today. Again there are problems with this theory. Among these are the Moon's density, the fact the far side of the Moon has a thicker crust than the near side, certain elements found on the Moon, etc.

The newer theory, that the Moon is the result of a natural "georeactor" near the equator on Earth that exploded, so the Moon and was thrown off into space when the Earth was still very young, has been promoted to compensate for problems with the impact theory. However, this theory, too, has problems, so much so, that most scientists still seem to prefer the impact theory despite its flaws.

So today, scientists simply don't know for sure how the moon came to be in our skies. Every few decades, they come up with a different idea of how it could be, it seems. For a short while, each of these seems to be the prominent theory, before a newer one then eclipses them. Then they are, for all practical purposes, discarded. These newer theories, in their turn, then try to answer the problems of the last one, and somehow account for them.

This seems to be the real history of our moon, an ongoing effort to account for the thing, how it came to be in our skies. To date, we've only been partially successful in this effort, because we simply can't explain all the odd things about our Moon, no matter what theory we choose. Each one lacks credibility in some fashion or another.

One of the theories about the Moon is that the earth simply captured it at some point in its early history. This idea accounts for much about the Moon being here, but it, too, has serious problems. It can't account for the nearly circular orbit, for instance, among other things, like the density, angular momentum of the Moon, etc.

Another theory is the Moon formed along with the Earth from the same dust cloud. This works well for explaining the similarity in materials of each world, and the age of it, as compared to Earth. They were born together from the same "stuff." Nevertheless, the theory doesn't work in other ways, either, because of a number of things. Again, the angular momentum is wrong, the orbit is wrong, and the fact one side of the Moon's crust is thicker than the other is, and so on.

Another and very glaring problem with this theory is the Moon's core is too small compared to the Earth's. They should be more in proportion. Additionally, there is that nasty little density problem again, the Moon's density is too low for its size and relative to Earth's density. The orbit around the Earth is wrong for this theory, as well. Besides this, the theory, too, doesn't explain how the difference for elements on the Moon's surface (titanium, neptunium, etc.) came to be, compared to those on Earth.

7. **Spaceship Moon Theory.** There is one theory that does account for how the Moon came to be in our skies, and it answers *all* the questions, solves all the problems of the other five theories combined. Unfortunately, this is the one theory that mainstream scientists simply do not wish to entertain as a plausible idea, at least, not most of them.

Admittedly, it does seem a far-out idea at first glance. Nevertheless, nonprofessionals did not come up with this idea. Rather, the theory is the product of two, well-respected, mainstream scientists, ones esteemed by their peers of the time.

They came up with this startling idea, the Spaceship Moon Theory, otherwise known as the Hollow Moon Theory.

Although, again, at first glance, this theory seems outrageous, it does answer all the issues of our other current theories—all of them, amazingly. The Spaceship Moon theory, which is also sometimes referred to as the Vasin-Shcherbakov Theory, so named for the two Soviet scientists who first proposed it, says that our moon could be artificial, to some degree, at least. The theory further states the Moon was deliberately maneuvered into orbit around the Earth by extraterrestrials at some time in our past. The two scientists, Michael Vasin and Alexander Shcherbakov, proposed this idea in an article *"Is the Moon the Creation of Alien Intelligence?"* This article was published in July 1970. Both scientists were respected members of the Soviet Academy of Sciences.

These two researchers proposed the idea the moon had been hollowed out, to some degree. Just how much, is a matter of conjecture and argument, with different people going for different amounts of space inside the moon, as having been hollowed. The moon would have a natural (almost natural), rocky surface, an inner metal shell at some depth, and a means of propulsion, probably one as yet unknown to us humans, but possibly fusion power.

This last is mentioned, because there have been reports of blue glows on the Moon. Spectral analysis of the blue glows by one researcher showed them to be virtually identical to the light given off by fusion reactions in experiments here on Earth. This implies the blue glows might be generated by such fusion reactions. These glows are much more common than one might think! Aristarchus Crater has had blue glows reported in and around it for so long, that the crater has received the nickname by astronomers of "the Blue Gem."

Again, this theory of a Spaceship Moon, or Hollow Moon, although seemingly beyond the scientific pale, does account for virtually every problem we have with the Moon. It accounts for:

a. The extremely circular orbit of the Moon.

b. The fact the three outer layers of the moon's surface seem to be reversed, which goes contrary to the normal theories of how geology works, where here on Earth, denser layers of material always settle to the bottom, and the lightest are on top. Yet on the Moon, this is the opposite. That's because of the hollowing effort these scientists claim, and the dumping of lower layers onto the surface.

c. The theory explains the seemingly two-low density of the moon. Since part of it may be hollow, this would account for the why the moon does not seem to be as dense as it should be for its size.

d. The Spaceship Moon Theory explains all the odd things that have been seen on the moon. In NASA's own report, "A Technical Report NASA TRR-277," commissioned back in the early 1960s on translunar phenomena, cited many strange sightings over the centuries, ones claimed seen on the surface of the moon. Astronomers and observers, dating back some five hundred years for the purposes of the report, have seen everything from blinking lights, strange tracks on the surface, "streaks," blue glows, flashing beacons, strange mists, vapors, clouds, glowing objects moving about the surface of the moon, "lightning," as well as even volcanoes erupting. Since scientists feel certain there aren't any active volcanoes on the moon, this last just couldn't be. It's rather unlikely, as well, that there would be lightning without an atmosphere to conduct such.

Nonetheless, many observers and famous astronomers have noted over the years something that looked very much like the glow of volcanic eruptions on the moon. Sometimes, these are not short-lived phenomena, but go on for days, weeks, months, and even sometimes for several years! Therefore, something seems to be happening on our Moon, and it isn't volcanoes. If not, the glaring question remains, just what is happening? What is it we are seeing?

e. The proponents of the Spaceship Moon Theory also point to the fact the large craters on the moon are relatively shallow, while smaller ones have the normal depth one would expect for such size. They argued the reason for this was the inner metal shell they theorized for the moon. Small meteor impacts made normal-sized craters. Larger impacts struck deeper into the moon's surface, rebounded off the inner shell, and so created a flatter and shallower center to the larger craters.

f. The authors also say their theory would explain some of the minerals found on the surface of the moon. These include zirconium, titanium, and chromium. These are in amounts considerably larger than are found on earth, especially titanium. In addition, titanium can only be refined at extremely high temperatures, temperatures we've only recently achieved ourselves here on Earth in the last century.

Yet, the moon seems to have a relative abundance of titanium on the surface by comparison to here on Earth. How is this possible? No current theory of the formation of the Moon and Earth accounts for such extremely high temperatures as being a naturally occurring thing.

g. Therefore, the authors of the Spaceship Moon Theory also claim this has been done artificially. They also point to the fact there is Neptunium on the moon. Neptunium is a radioactive isotope with a relatively short half-life of only 2.14 million years. By this point in time, after supposedly some four and a half billion years, there should be little if any Neptunium left on the moon. This is the way it is here on Earth. There is almost no natural Neptunium for any practical purposes. So how do we account for Neptunium still being on the moon, when it should long ago have degraded to a more stable element, just as it has done here on Earth?

Then, too, there is a large quantity of Helium-3 on the Moon. Scientists have a hard time accounting for this, as well, since on

Earth, Helium-3 is extremely rare. helium-3, by the way, is a perfect fuel for fusion reactions, as it turns out. This is just one more odd coincidence in a string of them when it comes to our Moon.

Other researchers have promoted the Spaceship Moon Theory as well. Don Wilson was one of them. He published, *Our Mysterious Spaceship Moon* in 1975. He went to great lengths to find many more supporting facts for the idea of the Spaceship Moon Theory being true and seems to have accomplished his goal. His arguments were clear and telling.

The following year, George H. Leonard also published a book with photographs of the Moon, which, when enlarged, seem to show huge pieces of machinery in some of the photographs. Although for the purposes of this book, the photos seemed rather vague and insubstantial in some respects, so therefore subject to several interpretations as to what they might depict, others did certainly look like machines of some sort.

h. If the Moon has been here for most of Earth's history, there is the question of the number of meteorites from the Moon found here on Earth. In total, they comprise around fourteen pounds, or less, and almost the same amount as the number of Martian meteorites found here on Earth. This is odd, very much so. The Moon is only 402,336 kilometers from Earth. Mars, however, is about 54,717,696 kilometers away, and that is at its closest approach to us, which has yet to happen. So far, throughout human recorded history, that close an approach has not yet occurred. Normally, Mars is more in the neighborhood of 93,341,952 to 99,779,328 kilometers from us.

i. Furthermore, the Moon's surface is incredibly pockmarked with impact craters, large and small. The far side of the Moon is even more so in this regard. Mars, although having its share of craters doesn't have anywhere nearly as many. Some of this may be due to erosion, since Mars does have an atmosphere where the Moon does not. Yet, the atmosphere of Mars is incredibly thin, and so its winds are very weak and do little in the way of erosion.

Additionally, it doesn't rain on Mars, so for billions of years, there has been no water erosion to speak of due to this. There is evidence of some water coursing over the land in places in the far past, and perhaps some small amount of water still manages to melt in the permafrost of Mars on occasion and flow on the surface, but only for very short periods of time, mere minutes in most cases, probably. Mars was once a wet world, but that was a very long time ago. For the last couple of billion years, it has been a dying planet when it comes to any forms of life. The most researchers hope for is to find some type of microbial life on Mars, at best.

Even so, this doesn't nearly come close to accounting for why the Moon has just so many more craters than Mars. The Moon literally has craters within craters, within craters! This tells us some of these are far older, since the same regions have been struck again after the original strikes.

However, we aren't concerned as to why there is this great discrepancy between Mars and the Moon in number of craters here, but rather the consequences of it. We have the Moon just a scant 402,336 kilometers away, so close to us, we've landed men on it a number of times. The Moon has suffered major impacts repeatedly and seemingly constantly, if one goes by all those craters everywhere on its surface. One would logically think impacts on the Moon would send more debris to Earth than Mars would, because the Moon is so much closer. Yet again, we find about the same amount of meteorites by weight, in total, here on Earth for both Mars and the Moon.

How can this be? Mars should have far fewer meteorites reaching the Earth than the Moon, because it is so very much farther away. Logic would dictate this would be so. So how do we explain this, the fact both worlds have sent us about the same number (in weight) of meteorites?

Some researchers claim they have the answer. They say this situation exists because the Moon has only arrived in orbit around the Earth relatively recently in our history. In other words, there just hasn't been enough time yet for meteorites from the Moon to accumulate in greater quantities than those from Mars. The Moon is playing "catch-up," as it were.

As one can see, there are problems, therefore, with all the main origin theories of the Moon. The Moon Capture Theory, The Accretion Theory, The Fission Theory, The Impact Theory, and the Georeactor Theory all have key issues/problems. Some have trouble with the Moon's current circular orbit. Some have trouble with the Moon's density. Others have problems with the too-high incidence of certain elements on the Moon, such as the titanium and neptunium issues mentioned above. Some can't account for the similarity in the isotopic ratio of material from the Moon compared to that of Earth's. The Fission Theory, which dates back to Darwin's time, claimed the Pacific Basin was where the Moon came from, but we now know that just isn't so. Instead, the Pacific Basin is the result of continental drift.

Therefore, as outlandish and improbable as it may seem to be by some, The Spaceship Moon Theory is actually plausible for this reason. (Too see a much more in-depth analysis of this theory, please see, *For The Moon Is Hollow And Aliens Rule The Sky*—the prequel to this book.)

Still, if this theory is true and there is a good possibility it just may be, then what? What if the Moon is an interloper into our skies, and not something that has always been there? What is it doing here? How has it affected our Earth? Do we have any other evidence for the idea other than the Moon's strangeness, itself?

Well, if we are to accept the idea the Moon hasn't always been in our skies, than its arrival must have been "something" to see for anyone who was alive at the time. Furthermore, there had to have been repercussions. One doesn't go around slinging objects the size of the Moon about the Earth, without this happening. Moreover, shouldn't there then be some sort of historical evidence for such a thing having occurred? Finally and perhaps most importantly, why and when did the Moon arrive here?

As good as the idea of the Spaceship Moon Theory is on its own in answering the fact the Moon is, for all practical purposes, an alien interloper in our skies, it is still just a theory. Yes, the idea does answer a lot of questions about our extraordinary moon, but we need other corroborating evidence. Unbelievably, there is also some of that, as well, it seems.

8. **Recorded History—A Time Before The Moon?** There is a good deal of evidence that humans remember a time when there was no Moon in the sky, or "before the Moon," as many of them put it. This evidence comes from a variety of sources, both written records, and oral ones, which would seem to further enforce the idea, to corroborate the theory of an Invader or Spaceship Moon. Multiple sources are always better than relying on just one source in such matters. When it comes to evidence, the more there is, and the more diverse it is, the better. However, exactly what are those sources? Well, let's take a look at some of them.

9. **The Moon Arrives at the Time of the Great Flood.** As partial support for our Invader Moon theory, according to some legends, it is said the Moon did not appear in the skies above us until around the time of the so-called Great Flood. One researcher, Henry Kroll, actually claims a specific year. It is his contention, based on his research; the Moon arrived in orbit around the Earth some 11,713 years ago. That is very close to the 12,000 figure that keeps cropping up in all sorts of ways with regard to human history.

Again, this idea of Mr. Kroll knowing an exact date may sound really "out there," and I have not seen the evidence for how he arrived at such a specific year, but in other respects, he does build a good case for his contentions, whether his time for the Moon's arrival is really that exact or not. Furthermore, other investigations seem to indicate it was just about 12,000 years ago, as well, that something cataclysmic took place on Earth, a major, worldwide event. Was this because of the arrival of the Moon?

There are recorded references to a time when the Earth was "moonless," a number of them, which tend to back the idea of the Moon not always having been here. Here are just some:

10. The Greeks. Aristotle tells of a time when there was no Moon, that the skies were "Moonless." As we all know, Aristotle was a revered and honored academic of ancient Greece. And when talking about a "Moonless" time, Aristotle referred to a people that lived in Arcadia. This was before his people, the Hellenes, had migrated to the region and settled there, so even by his own standards of the day, this was a very ancient time.

Aristotle claims the Pelasgians were the existing race dominating the area when the Moon's arrived. He said these Pelasgians lived in Arcadia at a time "before the Moon." Aristotle called these people Proselenes, which means, "Those before there was a Moon."

Aristotle was not alone. Two other prominent Greeks spoke of the Proselenes, as well. Both Anaxagoras and Democritus mention them as being "before the Moon" people, as well. So convinced were they of this fact, they had no problem relating this as a standard history lesson to their students of the time. In other words, they taught it as a truth of history and not just a myth or legend. Apollonius of Rhodes also talks of these pre-Moon people, as well, and in much the same vein.

Therefore, it would seem Greeks, the learned ones at least, were convinced there was a time when there were humans, but there was no Moon in the sky, for they talk of a time:

"when not all the orbs were yet in the heavens...and only the Arcadians lived of whom it is said that they dwelt on mountains... before there was a Moon."

11. The Romans. Nor were the Greeks alone in these beliefs. Much later, no less than the famous Ovid said:

"The Arcadians are said to possess their land before the birth of Joseph [Biblical Joseph], and the folk is older than the Moon."

This use of a reference to a biblical figure is interesting, because it helps us to determine the time this was supposed to have been. If we go by this statement, we know that a moonless time had to occur before the liberation of the Jews from Egypt, at least, and so in the very ancient and early times of that empire, but probably much further back in time than even that.

Hippolytus, a theologian of Rome in the third century also speaks of this when he says:

"Arcadia brought forth Pelasgus, of greater antiquity than the Moon."

Again, we have these references to a time long ago, a "greater antiquity."

Plutarch, as well, spoke about the time before a Moon in his *The Roman Questions*, when he stated:

"There were Arcadians of the Evander's following, the so-called pre-Lunar people."

Here, we hear just a little doubt creeping in on Plutarch's part, as he uses the term "so-called."

Censorinus also talks of a time where there was no Moon, and the night sky *"was moonless."*

Nor are such references to a time before there was a Moon restricted to just the Old World, because other cultures around the world also speak of such a moonless time in their ancient history. Since the foundation of this book is that whatever happened around 12,000 years ago was worldwide, at least some of these should be mentioned, as well.

12. The Americas. Adding even more support to the idea the Moon as not always having been here, as being a relatively recent arrival and that there was a "time before a Moon," there are the Mayans. The Mayans venerated Venus as the main nightly celestial body. It took precedent over everything else. The Mayans refer to a time when there was yet no Moon to rival the glory that was Venus, and Venus dominated the night sky. To the end of their civilization, it was Venus, the Mayans focused on and they used their superior mathematical capabilities to precisely make predictions about the orbit of that planet, where and when it would appear in the skies for the entire year, and for years to come.

The Columbian tribe, the Cordilleras, is another group of people who believed there was a time when there was no Moon. They always, to this day, start their stories of ancient times with the phrase:

"...before the Moon inhabited the night sky."

This is the same for the Chibchas tribe, as well, who use the phrase:

"...in the earliest times, when the Moon was not yet in the heavens."

In Bolivia, there are hieroglyphics, or more precisely, pictographs at Tiahuanaco, which blatantly state that the Moon did not arrive in the heavens until about 12,000 years ago. Again, that references to a certain time, 12,000 years, keeps cropping up, repeatedly now.

It must be said that having so many tales of a "time before there was a Moon" from around the world, and in recorded history from such places as diverse as Greece, Rome, Columbia, and Bolivia, does say something for the idea there might have been a time before there actually was a Moon in our skies.

Notice something else in all these comments of various ancient peoples about the Moon; they do not ever say anything like "before there was Mars in the night sky," or "before there was Venus in the night sky." Only the Moon gets singled out as not having been there. This is an amazingly consistent feature in all these statements by ancient peoples from around the world.

Just why is this? Why would people single out the Moon, but not any of the other planets? Why would the Mayans place such emphasis on Venus, which without the Moon, would be the most dominating feature of the night sky? Was the Moon not there at one time?

Therefore, because of the sheer number of them, such historical written records and oral comments should be given some real credence. After all, when people as diverse as the ancient Greeks and tribes in Bolivia, for instance, agree on such a thing as a time when there was no Moon, the idea deserves some real consideration.

There is another oddity about all this, as well. If the Moon has always been there, then we should see this mirrored in the religious and/or cultural works of many ancient civilizations around the world. We do, until one begins to go further back in time. Then, symbols of the Moon quickly seem to peter out. The further back we go in history, the more this becomes so.

13. A Lack of Ancient Moon Maps. Another possible and interesting piece of evidence for a time before the Moon is the startling lack of Moon maps from truly ancient cultures. Leonardo Da Vinci did a comprehensive one in 1505 CE, but other than that, depictions of the Moon in the form of maps are indeed rare, and even more so the further back in time we go.

This is unusual, because like the Sun, the Moon can be used to tell the seasons, since it, too, rises and sets at various points along the horizons in a repeat pattern that includes the solstice points. In addition, considering the Moon is by far the brightest and most dominating thing in the nighttime sky, one would have thought it would have precedence second only to that of the Sun in calendars. It does not. In fact, besides the Sun, it would seem that the constellation of Orion is the next big feature, and/or Venus, as with the Mayans. Just why this is, is a mystery.

One scientist was extremely puzzled by all this. A professor at the University of Western Ontario in Canada, Philip Stooke, an asteroid mapper, couldn't understand how this could be. As he put it:

"I simply could not believe this. I felt there just had to be an older map somewhere [of the Moon than the Da Vinci one]."

Well, after considerable research, Dr. Stooke did find such a map. He discovered a lunar map at an ancient site that dates back some 5000 years, or close to the time modern civilization began its start. This was in a tomb in Knowth, Ireland. However, that was the oldest reference to the Moon he could find.

One other researcher claims a cave painting in Lascaux, France, shows the Moon and this is said to be approximately 15,000 years old. This is rather a fluid date, and is not precise, but just an estimate. Furthermore, upon viewing the image, one is hard pressed to know for certain what it is, let alone the Moon. Nothing older than that has ever been found, although there seem to be plenty of ancient depictions of the Sun to be found around the globe.

These are mainstream researchers, and like others, they wonder at this incredible dearth of such lunar images, the lack of ancient lunar calendars, and any reference to the Moon in the stone circles around the globe. Just why is this?

Again, next to the Sun, the Moon is the most prominent and therefore obvious choice for such things as determining seasons. Even our word, "month" is derived from "moonth," and simply by counting the number of "moonths" anyone can get a good idea of what time of year it is, certainly good enough to know when to plant crops, etc.

Nonetheless, for some reason, in ancient times, the Moon was not used in this way much, and further back, there was a time when it was not used at all! So one has to wonder, was the Moon just not there at one time? Was it a later intruder into the night skies, and so even after its arrival, wasn't trusted to be a part of the many calendars and such for telling time of year? Were those ancients afraid it might just leave again?

Once more, we have this dating of events back to around the time of 12,000 years ago. Again, we have evidence of something strange at or near the time of the ending of the last great glacial period on Earth. One then has to wonder if not all this is somehow connected, the ending of the glacial period, the references to a time before there was a Moon, the Great Flood, etc.

One has to ask, does it mean the Moon really is an interloper, an invader in our skies? Did our satellite world really come to us not nearly so long ago as cosmologists think? It seems this could well have been the case. Remember, the evidence comes from a variety of sources:

a. The Spaceship Moon Theory, again, a valid theory put forth by two renowned mainstream scientists. The Spaceship Moon Theory does explain many very peculiar attributes of the Moon. This even includes those maria we see on the side of the Moon facing the Earth, but that satellite having none on the far side. According to those scientists, the maria are there because they are the result of the interior being made molten and then pumped out onto the surface of the Moon and so becoming such huge frozen lava fields. This would explain yet even another oddity of the Moon; the near side of the Moon's crust is thicker than the far side of the Moon. If the pumped material was deposited on the near side, this would make the crust there thicker than other places.

b. Furthermore, to corroborate this theory further, we also have the historical written records of various civilizations that all clearly refer to a truly ancient time "before there was a Moon."

c. We also have the orally handed down traditions in many cultures, whose ancient stories often begin with "before there was a Moon," or "in a time before the Moon."

d. In addition, when one realizes that all these cultures and civilizations talk about the Moon this way, but not Mars, Venus, or Jupiter, Saturn, or whatever, which would seem more likely candidates than something as close as the Moon is to us, one has to wonder about such consistency of choice. Why always the Moon being new, but not the other planets visible to the naked eye? Why always is it the Moon that is the Johnny-come-lately?

e. The lack of any pictorial diagrams or images of the Moon in ancient times.

f. The low number of lunar meteorites one Earth, being just the same amount as from far away Mars. If the Moon arrived late in our history, then there simply wasn't enough time for more meteorites to have come from our satellite.

When one considers all this, the huge number of lunar oddities, all of which can be answered by the Spaceship Moon Theory, the written records, the oral records, the fact there seems no portrayals of the Moon in truly ancient times, the low, lunar-meteorite count, one has to give the idea of an Invader Moon some real credence.

Still, if the Moon is a relatively recent trespasser into our night skies, what happened when it arrived? Shouldn't there have been some consequences for such a momentous occurrence? If there were, shouldn't there be some evidence of this to be found today? Additionally, is there is such evidence of such an event, doesn't that, in turn, further bolster the case for a Spaceship Moon invading our skies? If momentous events occurred, wouldn't this help tell us when the Moon did arrive?

Well, there seems to be some evidence to help us answer this question, as well. In fact, it's rather obvious with all the references and allusions made to the "when" part of it throughout this book so far. That date of 10,000 BCE., 12,000 years ago has just kept coming up time after time. Whenever we move back along the timeline, turn back the hands of the clock far enough, we seem to keep running into events occurring around this date. So just what did happen 12,000 years ago? What events unfolded that might further corroborate the idea of an Invader Moon? In the final chapters, we will discuss this.

CHAPTER 18

ALIEN BASES ON THE MOON?

For decades, conspiracy theories have run rampant about alien bases on the moon. This is with good reason. There seems to be a lot of evidence to suppose such a thing might actually be. Moreover, it is relatively recent evidence of the last few decades. Why are we interested in this? Well, if our theory of and Invader Moon is correct, then there should be signs of extraterrestrial activity on the moon, now, but even more importantly, in the past.

Most of us who delve into these subjects know about a lot of the evidence put forward by various people, including former workers at NASA, independent researchers, and even some astronauts. Despite this, many people remain unconvinced. Therefore, do we have more recent evidence for aliens on our Moon? Again, it seems we do, and this evidence doesn't come from our own government.

1. **Recent Evidence For Aliens On The Moon.** Most of us know the Chinese have been making strides in their own space program. This alarms some of us, but it is probably a good thing. We need other governments and even independent commercial enterprises to get involved in traveling into space.

Otherwise, and despite many triumphs of NASA, we're limited to just one resource for knowing about what is "out there."

That's not good enough. This single source, primarily, is responsible for the creation of all the conspiracy theories, because people feel NASA and/or our government is hiding the facts, or at least some of them. So I think it's a good thing other countries are getting involved in space, as well. With the Chinese we have some interesting information.

After orbiting a satellite around the Moon, the Chinese released some interesting photos. These show objects that do not appear to be natural. In other words, they appear artificial. Moreover, they are not the product of humans, apparently, unless NASA has really been lying to us! Therefore, one has to assume "somebody else" made them. This sort of thing is not new. For decades, photos have been leaked of what looked to be abandoned bases, old ruins, and even some structures that appear still occupied. Our Moon seems to have more life on it than anyone would have thought possible 50 years ago, if these photos are real. Moreover, many people believe these alien bases are conniving with our government to take over Earth in one form or another.

If this sounds unbelievable to you, then I would refer you to Mr. Milton Cooper. He was a naval intelligence officer with a security clearance. Mr. Cooper insists that not only do aliens have bases on the Moon, but also some of them are operational. One base in particular, referred to as "Luna," is even conducting mining as we speak, according to him. Mr. Cooper also states this base, on the far side of the Moon, is also home for a number of alien spacecraft, more commonly known as "mother ships." He has more to say. He adds these larger ships are seldom used to come to Earth, but rather smaller, more shuttle-like saucers are used instead.

2. **Alien Bases On Far Side Of The Moon**. One of the most constantly recurring themes among UFO conspiracy theorists is the idea that there are alien bases on the far side of the Moon. This debate has raged for decades. Those who believe in the idea point to various photographs released by NASA.

These are untouched photographs and some do actually seem to show weird things on the surface of the far side of the moon. Of course, there are also the inevitable hoaxes. Why some people persist in doing this and muddying the waters on this subjects is beyond understanding, frankly.

However, if one does look at the original NASA photographs, rather than the enhanced versions, again, there are still some peculiar images. In addition, we have strange the tale of Karl Wolfe. The man swears his story is a true one. If so, it is compelling.

The Director of Intelligence employed Mr. Wolfe at the time the events allegedly occurred, for the Headquarters Tactical Air Command. This was for the Technical Division. He worked at Langley Field, in Virginia, a secure facility. While he was there, they were receiving data from the Lunar Orbiter Project. Langley was where the data was turned into actual images. He was one of two such operatives.

While working there, he was ordered to troubleshoot some problems they were having with some equipment. This was over in a military lab on the base, one run by the NSA. It was a highly secured facility. Mr. Wolfe further claims that at the time, he had no idea what the NSA actually was. Remember, this is back when NASA was still trying to find a location for the first Apollo landing on the moon. The images transmitted to Langley Field, were supposedly to aid in picking the precise location for landing.

Carl responded to the request and went over to the lab. In order to do this, though, he had to have his security clearance raised temporarily. At the time, he thought this was no big deal. However, when he entered the facility, a large hangar, he was surprised to see many people working there, more than he had imagined. Furthermore, they seemed to be working in an almost frenzied state.

He was also surprised to find quite a number of foreign people there. Now, all the excitement of everyone rushing around him, and with so many people being there, he found the atmosphere contagious. He became tense. He also began to think what he was working on might be more important than he had originally imagined.

After examining some equipment in the special dark room, he realized it would need repairing off-site. He would be in charge of repairs. As he waited, he entered into a conversation with someone who worked there. One of the first questions he asked was why the transformation of the incoming data being turned into imagery was not at NASA in Houston, Texas.

The military worker's response was that all the imagery was downloaded. They then turned these into photographs for researchers to study, including various members representing different branches of the American military. The reason for this was early images had shown bizarre objects on the moon, structures. These were obviously artificial in nature. Someone intelligent had built them. Specifically, what seemed to concern the researchers most was what appeared to be a type of base on the far side of the moon. Again, this was according to the technician.

At first, Mr. Wolfe found this hard to believe, but the technician was adamant in saying it was true. More was to come. Although not actually stated, the worker strongly implied the base was not of human origin. To demonstrate his veracity, the technician showed actual photographs of the base. For Karl Wolfe, there was no doubt in his mind that he was actually looking at artificial structures. These obviously were not craters, mountains, ridges, or chasms of any sort. They were too geometrically precise. In addition, Mr. Wolfe was all too aware that humans simply couldn't have made them. He knew humanity did not yet possess the capabilities for such a feat.

One of the features that particularly drew his attention was what looked like very standard arrays of radar antennae. They resembled closely those already existing on Earth. At first, he wondered if America's enemies have built these things, but knew this was impossible. America was in the midst of a Cold War with Russia, true, but the Russians were demonstrably behind the United States' space program. They had yet to even orbit a man around the Moon, let alone land one on that satellite. No, this had to be someone else, someone from "out there."

With this realization came fear. Now he understood why there were so many foreign representatives in the hangar. He also realized something else; he wasn't supposed to have seen these photographs. He was undoubtedly in violation of his security clearance by having done so.

Mr. Wolfe realized he faced not only losing his job, but he could well be arrested and tried. The penalties for treason and espionage were great. At this point, he just wanted to repair the equipment and get on with his life, and not even think about what he had seen.

This was easier said than done. Yes, getting on with his work was no problem, but trying to forget what he had seen was considerably more difficult. Still, fear kept him in check. He didn't say anything to anyone about what he'd seen. He finished his service, honoring his security clearance oath. Mr. Wolfe maintained his silence after his discharge.

However, he could not do this forever. As time passed, and more information leaked out about UFOs and government cover-ups, Karl Wolfe finally felt he had to say something, go public with what he had seen and known. This was 30 years after he had witnessed the photographs.

The interesting thing about all of this is that Mr. Wolf had little to gain by going public, and he risked a lot. Remember, he was violating his security oath. What little notoriety he might get by telling the world what he had seen was outweighed by the danger of his being arrested and tried for violation of his security oath.

There are several other things to remember about this story, as well. First, Mr. Wolfe consistently insists he was telling the truth. Secondly, he did work at the facilities he claims to have, and did have security clearances at the time he was supposed to have had them.

Combined with the danger he placed himself in by going public, the harmful consequences such an action might engender from the government, would make it seem more than reasonable that Mr. Wolfe was telling the truth as he saw it. It is for this reason this particular case is mentioned here. The story of Mr. Wolfe is definitely one of the most reliable ones researchers have come across.

3. **NASA Employee Clark McClelland.** Clark McClelland, who worked for NASA, declared in a public online posting on July 29, 2008, that he saw an extraterrestrial of extraordinary height (one of the giants of old?) a total of some 2.74 meters or so. He said the alien was in the Space Shuttle Bay and was busy conversing with several NASA astronauts. Apparently, he was there as an official monitor of one of the shuttle flights. This was at the Cape Canaveral Kennedy Space Center.

Fred Steckling, author of *We Discovered Alien Bases on the Moon II*, stated that based on informants and sources of his, including several who worked at the Department of Defense, as well as NASA that *"...there are buildings on the Moon. There is mining equipment on the Moon."*

Another point driven home by these people was there were bona fide NASA photographs of these structures. Hundreds of these are reported to exist. Moreover, many of these images have undergone alterations to hide artifacts/bases spotted on the Moon. Only then were the pictures made available to the public.

Furthermore, these sources say that all NASA missions have been watched or monitored by extraterrestrials, at least one species, but very likely more. This wasn't news to NASA, or at least, not after the initial discovery of aliens, which was before humans ever set foot on the Moon. So NASA officials weren't surprised, apparently, when the Apollo missions suffered from close flybys, not only on the way to and from the Moon, but while having landed there.

This was true even while some NASA craft were in orbit around our planet. Reports of such craft being buzzed by "alien vehicles," ones that *"flew within fifty feet"* sometimes of the Earth spacecraft. In fact, the author Fred Steckling also strongly suggests that astronaut "Buzz" Aldrin suffered a nervous collapse later in life, and this was not only directly due to what he had endured while on his missions, but also from ongoing pressure from various government agencies and individuals to keep him silent on what he had seen.

Still, we don't have just to rely on Buzz Aldrin. For instance, Astronaut Ed Mitchell, one of the astronauts who actually walked on the Moon, believes after careful consideration that there is sufficient evidence to believe the Roswell Incident actually took place. He feels there was a crash there, one made by some extraterrestrial space vehicle, and human recovery efforts did manage to find debris at that New Mexico site.

Although never having admitted to actually witnessing any sort of alien spacecraft, Mitchell states he met with officials/officers in and out of the military who openly declared to him that they knew alien artifacts existed, including technological ones, and they were or had been involved in dealing with such things.

He's not alone. Gordon Cooper, another astronaut, reportedly told a select committee of the United Nations that, virtually every day, unknown vehicles or objects invade American airspace, are subsequently picked up on radar, but their origin and makeup were completely unfamiliar. Moreover, he implied the technology of the things seemed such that to successfully shoot them down or intercept them was not really a viable option. In short, their capabilities were way beyond our own.

More than just American astronauts are dealing with UFO sightings. Of course, they seem to have the most, but then, the American Space Program has been far more vigorous than most other countries of the world, except perhaps, for Russia, especially while still the old Soviet Union. Here is what Cosmonaut Victor Afanasyev had to say about a 1979 flight to the Soyuz 6 Space Station:

"It followed us during half of our orbit. We observed it on the light side, and when we entered the shadow side, it disappeared completely. It was an engineered structure, made from some type of metal, approximately forty meters long with inner hulls. The object was narrow here and wider here, and inside there were openings. Some places had projections like small wings. The object stayed very close to us. We photographed it, and our photos showed it to be twenty-three to twenty-eight meters away."

Here again, we have the same sort of sightings of alien spacecraft, or at least those of unknown origin, trailing after human spacecraft, following and seemingly monitoring them. Whether American or Russian astronauts, these sorts of reports are amazingly similar, which lends credence to the idea all this is true.

Need still more proof? Here are some quotations by what can only be described as irrefutable sources:

"This 'flying saucer' situation is not at all imaginary or seeing too much in some natural phenomena. Something is really flying around. The phenomenon is something real and not visionary or fictitious."

The above quotation was from the Chief of the Joint Chiefs of Staff, and Chief of Staff of the United States Air Force, General Nathan Twining.

"Unknown objects are operating under intelligent control... It is imperative that we learn where UFOs come from and what their purpose is..."

—Admiral Roscoe H. Hillenkoetter and Director of the Central Intelligence Agency (CIA) from 1947 through 1950.

"...I've been asked about UFOs and I've said publicly I thought they were somebody else, some other civilization."

—Commander Eugene Cernan. Source is the *Los Angeles Times*, 1973 article.

"At no time, when the astronauts were in space were they alone: there was a constant surveillance by UFOs.

—Scott Carpenter, a former astronaut.

He purportedly took a picture of a UFO while orbiting the Earth. This was in 1962. The fact of his having sighted something and then photographing it is not really in dispute. However, NASA has never deemed it necessary to release such a photograph.

So it goes and continues to go. Thousands of reports of extraterrestrial spacecraft seen in our skies have been made.

Reports by astronauts and test pilots sighting objects while in Earth orbit, and/or on their way to and from the Moon are also numerous. Former officials at NASA, government officials of various departments, retired members of NASA, etc., also openly claim they have either seen photographs of objects on the Moon, such as spacecraft, what look like mining operations (principally on the far side of the Moon), and more.

The interesting part about all this as that some officials declare some of the bases appear to be in ruins, being pockmarked with small craters from meteor impacts. They appear abandoned, but not all. Some seem active. That the vacuum skies of the Moon are active with UFO sightings also seems real enough.

There is so much more, but there just isn't enough room to include it all here. Still, suffice it to say, there does seem to be plenty of real evidence, both in photographs and testimony by very trusted people, including astronauts, test pilots, government officials and more that not only do aliens exist, but the Moon seems to be one of "their" places. In fact, many conspiracy theorists argue this is why we haven't been back to the Moon for so many decades. They claim we were warned off.

One does have to wonder why over forty years have lapsed since we last landed on the Moon. Moreover, it is curious to note that when government officials do talk about going back, they invariably mention establishing bases on the far side of the Moon. A recent European Union government official said this would be a good thing to do. The Chinese, too, have publicly mentioned they would like a base on the far side of the Moon, as well.

Only the United States seems particularly leery of this idea. Oh, we talk about going back to the Moon. Former President George W. Bush even wanted to make it something of a priority. However, it never happened. In fact, nothing came of it, not even a feasibility study, it seems.

For some reason, we seem content these days to stay much closer to the Earth, as with the International Space Station (ISS). Either that, or NASA seems to be fixated on sending only robotic probes to other places, and these places aren't the Moon! Mars seems to be the new favorite, or Saturn and its moon, Titan, as well as the asteroid Ceres, the pluton, Pluto—well, any number of far-flung places in the solar system.

Yet, one of the most fascinating places, and the closest to us, seems to be of no interest to NASA any more, and there is still so much to learn about our Moon. For instance, as mentioned earlier, further investigation by manned expeditions to the Moon might actually arrive at the true origin of the Moon, whichever one of the six theories that might be. But no, we don't go there.

Occasionally, we send a satellite, as does China, or Russia, or even the European Space Agency, but nobody, except the Chinese, has landed anything more on the surface of the Moon. Even with the Chinese, it was just a small rover, and one that quickly ceased to function. This wasn't on the far side of the Moon.

So when we are drawn to the idea of going back to the Moon, it seems to be to the far side, or not at all. A curious state of affairs, it seems, because logistically, such a thing is more difficult to accomplish. At least, it is more so than having a base on the near side of the Moon. This is so both because of extra communication problems, but because of other factors, as well. Safe landing sites on the far side are harder to come by, because the far side is far more riddled with craters than the near side. Again, that's just another enigma of the Moon. There are so many, and yet we'd rather explore the outer system, all the way to Pluto and beyond, it seems, than to visit our so-close neighbor once more.

The question has to be asked why this might be so? NASA did experience a decline in public awareness and interest with its ongoing Apollo missions. The public began to get blasé about the whole idea of trips to the Moon. It was as if they were just another ho-hum event, which of course, wasn't so. Every trip took great effort and great risk on the part of the astronauts involved. The ill-fated Apollo 13 expedition is a good example of this.

However, it is understandable that due to declining public interest, as well as cuts in government funding, the agency's interest in the Moon might wane some. Some say the funding cuts were the primary cause, that with the winding down of the Cold War with the Soviets, it was no longer necessary to have the "space race."

This theory doesn't really work. The Cold War, rather than winding down at the time NASA cancelled the Apollo program, instead was heating up. The ensuing 1980s saw the greatest rivalry between the two superpowers, and more money was spent in that decade on the Cold War (by both sides) than at any time in the past. So this seems an unlikely explanation for the stopping of the space program. After all, he who controls the high ground controls almost everything.

In addition, as mentioned in another of my books, *For The Moon Is Hollow And Aliens Rule The Sky,* in real dollars, the International Space Station, so far, has been more costly in real dollars spent, than the entire Apollo Program. Therefore, the cost of the Apollo program simply couldn't be the overriding reason for its cessation, not when another and even more expensive project was started.

The next logical step in the space program by NASA, as far as the public, scientists, and most others were concerned, was to start a small base on the Moon. This never happened, much to the surprise of millions, if not billions. Instead, we created a small manned space station in near-Earth orbit, something that would not teach us much more than space shuttle flights could have accomplished if continued to be used in its place, and at far less expense.

No matter how one views this issue, even not taking into account the idea of extraterrestrial activity on the Moon as a reality, this is a very weird thing. We have the technology to put a base on the Moon. We have the means. Somehow, though, we are not motivated, at least, not on the government level.

Oh, we seem to be motivated and so can travel to Mars and clear out of the Solar System, but to put even a small research station on the Moon seems something we just don't want to do. Again, this is just strange.

The answer may just be that we've been warned off the Moon in no uncertain terms, or at least, certain areas of it. That could well be why we haven't been back to the Moon in almost half a century, despite vast improvements in our technology since the Apollo program, having developed far more efficient and thus cheaper methods of doing things, because our government has been told not to go back there. It makes one wonder; what will happen when private corporations achieve these same capabilities? What then? Will they somehow be stopped from going to the Moon? That time is coming very soon and so certain things may be made public, or some excuse for those companies not going to the Moon may be found, as well.

4. **The Black Knight Satellite.** Here, we have something that seems to add to our ancient alien and arrival of the Moon mystery. This is the Black Knight satellite. The first information about the so-called Black Knight Satellite dates back to 1954. Two separate newspapers, *The San Francisco Examiner,* as well as the *St. Louis Post Dispatch,* reported two satellites had been detected in polar orbits. This article was said to be the result of an interview with Donald Keyhoe, who claimed the United States Air Force had discovered these satellites.

It must be remembered that in 1954, nobody, not the United States or the old Soviet Union had launched any satellites at all. The space race really had yet to begin, and was still several years away. The implication was clear; someone not of this Earth was responsible for the satellites. Although the story did raise eyebrows, this was a short-lived phenomenon. Soon, the new story was forgotten and people went on with their lives.

However, in 1960, February of that year, *Time Magazine* said something else had been spotted. This was the result of a claim by the American Navy that it had spotted what they thought was a Soviet craft. A dark spacecraft was seen in a polar orbit. This, as it turned out, could not have been a Soviet satellite, so it had to have been something else. Then, in 1998 on one of the space shuttle missions, the STS-88 mission, again, an object was discovered and photographed. Newspapers at the time referred to the photos of that of an "alien artifact."

Of note also, is that not only the United States, but also the Soviet Union seemed very curious about whatever this object is that orbits our world in such an eccentric polar orbit. Furthermore, from the 1930s on, various astronomers have reported radio signals, which some claim come from this object. Photographs do keep popping up of it over the years. Dr. Luis Corralos, a member of the Venezuelan Communications Ministry took a photograph of the object in 1957. He was busy taking pictures of a Soviet satellite at the time.

In addition, the Grumman Aircraft Corporation also managed to take a photograph of the satellite. It then created a committee to investigate the object further. However, the results of this investigation were secret.

What exactly does the Black Knight Satellite have to do with our wanting proof of an ancient, technological civilization having been around some 12,000 years ago and earlier? Well, as it turns out, Astronaut Gordon Cooper, in 1963, spotted a greenish object. He reported this. To back his claim, the Muchea tracking station also confirmed there was an object, as well.

Then, an amateur radio operator picked up a transmission from the object, presumably the Black Knight Satellite. The signal, after decoding, was said to have been meant as a chart of the Epsilon Boötes, a double star system in the constellation of Boötes. The message is also supposed to have said the satellite came from there, and that it arrived in orbit around Earth some 13,000 years ago!

Now, normally, one would take such a thing with a large grain of salt, but the government's reaction to the discovery through all this time would seem to imply there is something to this information. For instance:

a. *Aviation Week And Space Technology* incurred the wrath of the Pentagon for publishing a story about the satellite. This was August 23, 1954. The Pentagon had not wanted the article published.

b. The keen interest in the Black Knight Satellite shown by both the US and the Soviet Union.

c. Also, the fact a committee was formed and Grumman Aircraft Corporation conducted an investigation after having photographed the Black Knight, *and then keeping the results secret.*

d. It is a story that won't die, with people over the decades getting radio signals from the object, photographing the object, and having radar tracked it.

The conclusion of all this is that there does seem to have been, and still is, a satellite orbiting our Earth in a strange orbit and that it has been there a long time. Apparently, it must be considered "untouchable" by our governments, because nobody seems to have interfered with it.

Or have they? There was the launch of our military's secret, unmanned space plane into orbit, and nobody in the public seems to know what it did up there in space for almost two years. Recently, it has been launched again. Absolutely no knowledge of what these several trips were for or why, has been forthcoming. The secret is a closely guarded one. So the question has to be asked, was one of its missions to observe the Black Knight Satellite and gather data on it?

Whatever the reason for the secret space plane flights, the Black Knight does seem to have been in orbit a long time. So long, in fact, it was reported before anyone on Earth had launched any types of satellites at all. Although it's hard to tell if the age of the satellite is true, according to that early radio operator, there are some interesting points about this aspect of things, as well.

1. Why would the Ham radio operator pick the particular constellation he did, if his story was a hoax?

2. Secondly, why would he claim a time of 13,000 years ago? This being so coincidentally close to the same time as all the events on Earth having occurred back then.

3. Furthermore, the radio operator picked this time long before we had any data to support the idea that something momentous occurred around that ancient time, even before researchers had even formulated the theory regarding some aspects of the of all this. The radio operator claimed a time that only *decades later* would have significance! Just a coincidence? Possibly, but if so it is a weird one, indeed.

Canadian Ex-Minister. Paul Hellyer, a former serving defense minister from 1963 through 1967 in Canada, has made some startling revelations in a speech he gave while visiting the University of Calgary. The minister, not known for being a radical or of the fringe element, claims that for thousands of years, extraterrestrials have been coming to our world. He even went on to say many of them were among us, but to tell them from humans was extremely difficult.

An article on this was published in the UK's *Daily Mail* as recently as April 22, 2015. In the article, they mention the minister claims there has been an ongoing cover-up by nations around the world with regard to this matter, and he feels it is time for them to divulge what they know.

Again, we have someone who was in high office claiming not only that UFOs are real, but also that they have been here for thousands of years. There is more evidence in this vein, but the evidence provided shows that:

1. UFOs are real, as are extraterrestrials.

2. They have been here for a long time, apparently thousands upon thousands of years, and...

3. They have had a great impact on us humans.

Consequently, if all this evidence isn't enough, one can find much more, including the prequels to this book. However, despite the fact there seems to be a preponderance of evidence to be found for the above ideas, it is understandable some will still refuse to admit the truth of all this. This is reasonable, considering how frightening that truth is...not everyone is up to handling it, it seems.

Still if scientists, astronauts, pilots, government officials, members of NASA, employees of NASA, foreign ministers of defense, photographs, and such, are not enough to convince one of the reality of all this, then perhaps nothing can. However, at some point, we have to move on with what we know. Now, with this chapter, we have all the pieces we need to put our puzzle together, get a general idea of what this is all about.

CHAPTER 19

ALL THE PIECES OF THE

PUZZLE

Do we have enough pieces of the puzzle to complete a picture of what the world was like 12,000 years ago and before, and also what happened to change all that? It would seem we do. Let's take a quick look at the pieces, once more, just to remind ourselves of what they are, since there have been so many of them. First, we must consider the sources of our evidence. Evidence in this book has been drawn from three principal sources:

1. **Physical or "Hard" Evidence.** This hard evidence comes from the sciences including geology, archaeology, and astronomy, among others. Remember, even the Spaceship Moon Theory is not mine, but was that of two prominent scientists of the Soviet Academy of Scientists.

2. **Written Historical Records.** This book has drawn heavily for evidence from not only actual recent history, but also the written records of a number of civilizations. If there was

"a time before the Moon," then this wasn't made up for the purposes of this book. It is "written" in the records of a number of civilizations as being true, and can be found by anyone who chooses to verify them.

3. **Oral Histories.** Where there were no written records, this book has relied upon oral traditions, the oral histories of various peoples around the world. Yes, some scientists consider these merely stories, and/or just legends or myths. For this reason, such "stories" were not included unless they came from more than one culture, were consistent in their assertions, and were very much the same, despite having come from different places around the globe. For example, any historian or archaeologist who has studied the matter at all readily admits that the "stories" of a Great Flood are worldwide and are remarkably consistent in their principle statements about the flood. The same holds true for there being "a time before there was a Moon." For this reason only, such oral statements are included in this book.

Besides all this, the book has used the following evidence sources, as well:

1. **Actual Physical Sites.** This book makes great use of information about actual physical sites, such as Arkaim, in Russia, the stone "forts" of Sardinia, the monuments of Carnac, France, the various sites of pyramids around the world, etc. These sites are not the product of a fevered imagination, but rather are real physical places anyone can visit and probably should, if they have an interest in this subject.

2. **Ooparts and Archaeological Discoveries.** This book placed emphasis on these because for ooparts, there are just so many that have been determined not to be hoaxes, as with the "screws" found in the Ural Mountains. What they are, archaeologists cannot account for, but they are not hoaxes. Despite this, it would appear archaeologists often prefer to

ignore ooparts. Again, this doesn't mean they aren't real, aren't tangible objects. The World Map Stone is a good example of this. Ignore it. Deny it. Do what one will, but it is real and ancient. It is "there."

3. **What Have We Found With All This Evidence?** Well, we've discovered there are many pieces to this puzzle. For starters:

A Piece Of The Puzzle. We have found archaeological evidence of super structures of stone, that even by many mainstream scientists' determinations, date back thousands of years before civilization is supposed to have begun. We have found these exist all over the world and are of strange origin. These massive constructions vary in size and shape, of course, but principally they consist of pyramids (worldwide), stone monuments of mammoth size (worldwide), tunnels and underground caverns (worldwide), and stone platforms of such dimensions that the word "massive" hardly is adequate to describe them. Even many mainstream scientists admit some of these predate our idea of when civilization began (approximately 3500 BCE) by thousands of years. Some even argue they are much older, and may date back 10,000, 12,000 or even 25,000 years ago. Other researchers argue they go back much further in time than even that.

How were these erected at a time when humans were supposed to have been either pure hunter-gatherer people with scarcely any other abilities at their command, or at most, living in small pocket settlements of less than a hundred on average? How could people who eked out a short existence with primitive agriculture do this? There is no evidence the people prior to the rise of our current civilization had the tools or the capabilities of erecting such mighty structures. To think people using stone tools and sticks built these things is absurd. How did they do this without any ability to write, to use mathematics, or without learned trades and talents in this regard? Such an idea is specious, at best.

Another Piece Of The Puzzle. As mentioned above, we have found evidence for a race of beings larger than ourselves and different from us in other ways. We have found evidence from multiple sources of beings that our human ancestors thought of as demigods or gods. Written record, after written record, as well as in oral histories from around the world all say the same things: These were beings from the sky.

All the stories, written and oral, also tell us these "sky people" were possessed of wondrous powers. They looked differently than us; although, some of them also might have been able to, on occasion, interbreed with us. Some of the sky beings helped us, but most did not. For the most part, all the stories and written texts (Sumerian, vedic, biblical), tell us that we acted as their servants of the temples (palaces), their beast in the fields, and their laborers in the mines if all these histories are even partially true.

Another Piece of the Puzzle. We have found evidence they had a greater cranial capacity than we have. We have even found more evidence that we humans, being in awe of them, tried to imitate their look, by deliberately elongating the skulls of some of our children. The old saying "imitation is the sincerest form of flattery" may not only be truer than we thought possible, but far older than we would have conceived of at one time.

We have written evidence the sky people, gods, demigods, aliens, demons, whatever name one wants to call them, who could fly about the world and into space. We also have the references in the *Epic of Gilgamesh* to the platform of Baalbek being a place where these beings ascended and descended from the sky with a sound like thunder, a roaring, and great volumes of smoke. The vedic texts of India talk of the same sort of thing.

Then there are the actual platforms, built by whom, mainstream archaeologists can only surmise, and for a purpose that simply can't be just to place a few temples on them. Who needs stone platforms that cover acres upon acres and are tens of meters thick for such a purpose? What primitive society would go to such huge lengths when they had neither the means, the necessary labor force, nor the time when their whole world was about a daily struggle just to survive? More to the point, where are those ancient temples? If the platforms survived so well for civilization after successive civilization to build their temples on them, where are the originals? Didn't those who built the platforms construct their temples to the same level of quality or expertise they did the platforms? That seems unlikely, if so.

Another Piece Of The Puzzle. We have evidence there well may have been more than one species. The Vedic texts talk of this with passages about the different types of demons. The Bible refers to "the Fallen, or the Watchers." The Sumerian texts refer to the Anunnaki. The Hopi refer to Ant People. So it goes and continues to go around the world. Everywhere, there are written records and oral stories of beings greater than us, ones who controlled, sometimes, guided, but often exploited us.

Images, written records, and more tell us that those who ruled us directly seemed very human-like in many ways, although being taller, stronger, more intelligent, and much longer lived. This was prior to the Great Flood.

We also have written, oral, and even physical evidence of a great war. This was a tremendous war, which may have been a "cold war" for a long time before it heated up. Radioactive skeletons in Mohenjo-Daro, an area of higher than normal radioactive land in India, as well indicate this was possible. Vitrified pottery, vitrified stone structures, and more, add to this idea's credibility. Craters along one latitude in North America show something struck there and caused great damage. Evidence of a "crown fire" that burned the forests in North America also indicates something catastrophic happened. The extinction at around the same time of the great species of mammals, the mammoths, great cats, giant sloths, and more, is another sign of some disaster, one that these giant mammals could not survive.

We have the vedic texts, which talk of horrendous explosions far brighter than the Sun, and which caused a poison to fall that killed thousands of soldiers. We have evidence from the Bible, the Sumerian cuneiform writings, etc., which speak of a great battle waged in the sky and on Earth. We have various legends from around the world that say the same. This sort of thing just goes on and on. To ignore such evidence would then seem to be shortsighted and pointless. Rather, it should be investigated more, and then incorporated into our world history, our timeline of human events.

Another Piece Of The Puzzle. We have evidence both written, and seemingly by mainstream scientists that the Moon is an interloper, a relatively recent invader in our skies. We have many references for this fact in the Greek, Roman, and New World cultures. We have, oddly, negative evidence, as well. We have the severe lack of any evidence of any reference to our Moon being there before a certain time in our history. We have the evidence of astronauts, government officials, and NASA officials that there are extraterrestrials, and they seem to buzz around the Moon like flies, with some officials even openly claiming they saw evidence of an ancient Moon base on the far side of the Moon. Photographs published also seem to indicate this could well be so.

Another Piece Of The Puzzle. Twelve thousand years ago. That magical date that just keeps coming up repeatedly, and in all sorts of different places in the investigations of various researchers. Repeatedly, we hear this date, this time mentioned, and referred to. It's as if 12,000 years ago was a major linchpin. It could well have been.

What do we know about this date? Well, the last glacial period of the Ice Age seems to have ended all too abruptly about then, 10,000 BCE. At the same time, the Monument Makers ceased their activities all over the world. The stories of giants trickled and then died after this point in time. Oh, we have the ancient stories of them, still, but discounting modern made-up fairy tales of the last two centuries, they seem to have all but stopped. The New Testament of the Bible, for instance has no stories of giants in the time of Jesus, or even well before.

Great places, some of mythic proportions, such as Atlantis, seemed to have vanished or stopped being used, as with Göbekli Tepe and others, around 12,000 years ago. Remember, Plato said it was 9000 years before his time, and he lived approximately 2500 years ago. This places the demise of Atlantis, if it existed, right around 10,000 BCE, again 12,000 years ago.

Another Piece Of The Puzzle. We have the legends of people fleeing to high places, onto rafts, arks, boats, etc. We have systems of caves, caverns and tunnels, whose purpose is now unknown to us, but which could well have been used for shelter from such a war. We have the vedic texts that tell of a great war, one involving over 400 species, battling it out in the air, on land, in the sea, in space, and yes, even one battle having taken place on the newly arrived Moon. We have similar accounts written in the Old Testament of the Bible, as well as remarkably consistent accounts of the same thing from around the world.

Another Piece Of The Puzzle. The Great Flood. Again, we have an event that seems to have physical evidence to support it really happened, and literally reams and reams of written records pertaining to such an incident. Then there are the countless oral traditions and native stories of such an event occurring worldwide. Did the Great Flood happen? It would seem it did. One thing is for sure, sea levels did rise and rise quickly and this great and rapid melting of the continental glaciers was triggered by "something."

Yet Another A Piece Of The Puzzle. After whatever occurred 12,000 years ago, after the finish of the great and catastrophic events, we have an abrupt cessation of the histories of beings such as the Nephilim or the Watchers, the Anunnaki, and of course those long-lived people mentioned in such places as the Old Testament and others, such as the *Sumerian List of Kings*. The time of 12,000 years ago seems not only to act as a marker for the end of one sort of time and type of civilization on our world, but the rise of another...us. Prior to this boundary layer, as one can think of it, the world was one way. Then came shattering events and the world after that was another.

Gone was one empire, whether one wants to call it the Rama Empire, the Empire of the Gods, Megalithia, or whatever, it ended. Civilizations vanished. Atlantis, it seems, along with the City Ys, and perhaps other cultures, sank beneath the waves. Again, worldwide massive monument building ceased abruptly. Contact between cultures was severed. The constant use of the Constellation of Orion in building projects ceased.

Everything seems to have changed and for good. What followed seems to have been the first Dark Ages, the first Great Interregnum, a stagnant period when humans were merely nomadic hunter-gatherers, or existed in tiny agriculture settlements, and scrabbled for a meager existence in the dirt, in the shadows of the great monuments that came before them. This, it seems, went on with little change for 6500 years, before civilization suddenly again found its footing and began to grow once more.

CHAPTER 20

THE PUZZLE IS COMPLETE

So **Just What Did Happen 12,000 Years Ago in 10,000 BCE?** Let's look at the complete picture. What we see is a grand and incredible sweep of events. To put them in order:

1. We have an ancient civilization, one that countless sources say ruled us humans and had existed for millennia or even more. Just how long it existed is something of a mystery. Much information states that in some fashion or another, it could have existed for a very long time, indeed. Atlantis may have been a part of it.

   Some think the total span of time for this civilization might even be millions of years. Others think the aliens came and went at different times throughout much of Earth's history, and so weren't always in residence here.
   These researchers think Earth was either a sort of waypoint on their journeys and/or a place of resources. This would account for the truly ancient mines discovered, for example. Proponents of the long-term theory also point to various ooparts discovered, as well as other pieces of evidence, such as the "cart" ruts on Malta and in Turkey, which date back several million years.

2. The evidence also seems to show the population of rulers of these ancient times was few in number, but had command of an impressive technology. *The Sumerian List of Kings*, as well as the Old Testament of the Christian Bible say the "kings" were incredibly long-lived, and so few in actual numbers. Nonetheless, many cultures speak of these ancients as having "magic" at their disposal. This would be science appearing to human primitives as magic.

3. There is also considerable evidence for there having been more than one race during the time before the Great Flood. Perhaps, some extraterrestrials were our rulers, even some may have wanted to help humans in some ways.

Nevertheless, it seems others, those "demons" of the ancient texts, did not want to help us. Instead, they chose actively to suppress us, or even exploited us for their own purposes. There is even some real evidence to suggest they tampered with our genome, may have even made us what we are today as modern humans. The Sumerian cuneiform texts speak of this. The earlier chapters in this book covering the Pre-Adamites explain this in more detail.

There is one more thing; in many cultures, including our own, there was an ongoing fight by some of the gods to give us knowledge, but for others, this was a terrible offense to commit. This adds emphasis to the idea there was friction among these different species of ancient aliens. In addition, different cultures do talk of more than one type of "demon" or alien, as with the Vedic texts saying there were over 400 different types.

4. Further evidence from many cultures and civilizations seems to suggest a great war was going on, a cold war, perhaps, at first. Vedic texts allude to this in some detail, as do other sources, as well, again as mentioned earlier in this book. There seems to have been an uneasy balance of power among these species, and this seems to have been not only on Earth,

but also as some texts say, involved other species and star systems, as well.

We have the constant references from all over the world of the Constellation of Orion, for instance, as being extremely important for some reason. The pyramids' placement on the ground mirrors that of the constellation in the sky. Carvings, inlays of artifacts, and stones also refer to Orion, as do many of the stone circles and monuments, as well. Therefore, it seems likely that not only were "things" going on here on Earth, but in space, as well, literally, and somehow, the constellation of Orion figured prominently in all this.

The best way to describe the situation seems to be, again, a balance of power of sorts. Judging by Sumerian texts, the Bible, etc, one species of them seemed to dominate the Earth. This was, apparently, the so-called Nephilim, Watchers, Anunnaki, whatever one prefers to call them. This gave them the upper hand. Then something happened, something momentous.

5. About 12,000 years ago, all this changed. Starting with the arrival of our Invader Moon and the effects extraterrestrial races had upon the Earth, everything seems to have gone to taken a dire turn for the worse. Humanity and those forerunner races would never be the same again.

The Moon appeared in our skies, as various written records say. The fact the Moon has many strange anomalies that standard origin theories for it have major problems, and that only the Spaceship Moon Theory answers them all, also seems to support the idea of an Invader Moon.

The arrival of our satellite would have caused physical disruptions on Earth, as that orb settled into orbit around our planet. Great tides would have occurred (origin of the Great Flood stories?) Earthquakes and even volcanoes took place. Civilizations, such as Atlantis ceased to exist. People died, both humans and those "others."

A true war broke out at this point, according again to historical records, both written and oral. We have physical evidence of some sort of celestial bombardment of the Earth, a time that—as the Bible referred to with Sodom and Gomorrah—can only be described as one of fire and brimstone. A global civilization that had once dominated the Earth, had worldwide communication and transportation, and one language, was reduced in large part to rubble or drowned by the seas.

Gone was a cohesive system of government. Gone was the ability to stay in communications with other regions of the planet. Survivors were isolated and defenseless. They had to seek shelter on mountaintops or underground. There is evidence there was some warning of what was to come, because tunnels, caves, and artificial caverns, as in China and elsewhere, were built. Perhaps, the approaching Moon was the warning for those who lived at the time. The surviving population would have to remain in such shelters for some time to come.

6. The bombardments then ensued, probably aided and abetted by whoever controlled the Moon. The Moon now occupied the high ground, ruled the skies. Those on that satellite, extraterrestrials, according to many astronauts, NASA officials, and more, commanded control over the Earth from this superior position. North America suffered devastation, as did Eurasia, and elsewhere. Meteor impacts striking water caused tsunamis. Coastal civilizations, already flooded, were flooded even more. Massive fires broke out, as in North America because of these impacts. Animals, entire species, became extinct. This may be where the legend of some animals surviving, thanks to the Ark (whether Noah's or whichever version one goes with), while others perished came about.

7. The worst was not over. The great glaciers, due to the bombardment, and perhaps at least a limited thermonuclear war, along with new tides created by the Moon were being torn apart, were in rapid retreat. Their waters were being released into the seas. Combined with the tides created by the Moon's arrival, flooding was a worldwide and major event, if one takes into account all the written and oral records of those

ancient times. Seas rose and land disappeared. Britain and Ireland were separated from Europe. Coastal areas flooded permanently. Land bridges sank beneath the waves. Isolated pockets of survivors were cut off from each other.

8. Again, events were not yet over. The equivalent of a nuclear winter now came into full force. Ash from fires, dust from explosions and impacts combined to dim the Sun for years. This devastated the earth, as well. This was the time of the continuing of the great die-off of large mammals. Over the next decades the woolly mammoth, the giant saber-tooth cats, the giant sloth, and many more animals would vanish forever.

Nor did the problems stop here. Despite this temporary chilling, the seas had risen with the rapid retreat of the glaciers. In a sense, the Great Flood continued. What had been dry land areas continued to be flooded. Low islands disappeared. All around the world, dry land was in retreat as the oceans expanded. Many who had taken refuge and shelter in caves, caverns, and tunnels and had thought they were safe from the fiery bombardment, now faced drowning from the rising tides.

The Pyramids and the Sphinx eventually found themselves by the seashore, engulfed by a shallow lagoon, as several archaeologists claim. The Black Sea was later created the same way, submerging surrounding settlements in the space of some thirty years.

It was around this time the Black Knight Satellite might have been launched. Was it to monitor events on Earth at a close range? Did it have a close-up view of just how badly damaged the civilization of the Nephilim/Watchers had become?

What of the ancient alien races on Earth? Records seem to indicate their day was over. They seem to have had few survivors, and they either abandoned Earth, or died here. Some records, as those speaking of the Nephilim, seem to indicate some left, a few then returned, and some just remained, but died out over time. The Great Flood marks the end of their reign on Earth. The extraterrestrials on the Moon had forced the giants of old, the Nephilim, to abandon the Earth or face being killed.

There is no doubt that what remained of intelligent species on the planet were mostly wiped out. Evidence for this can be found in the history of many cultures around the world. The Götterdämmerung had arrived, as the Norse called it, the dusk of the gods. The great battle of the gods, as the Greeks, Romans, and other cultures histories and oral traditions thought of it was over. As the Bible claims, only those of Noah's descent survived all this.

It is a contention of this book that, based on the written records of so many cultures around the world, there was probably more than one "Noah." Small groups of survivors probably each had their own leader who may have led them through all these catastrophes. In many cases, no doubt some form of rafts, boats, or other floating devices had to be used to reach dry land and escape the constantly rising waters. These leaders thus became the "Noahs" for their people and so around the world, the stories were all similar—small bands of people led by a leader survived a great flooding.

Additionally, all around the world, we have cultures that refer to people either emerging from caves and caverns after the Great Flood, or helped by other species that sheltered them below ground, and then brought them back to the surface when it was safe to do so, as with the Hopi Native Americans.

9. However, again, as to who won the war there can be no doubt. The losers were the Nephilim, the Anunnaki, the "Fallen," or whatever one wishes to call them. They vanished from the Earth. Those of the Spaceship Moon had won the day, but one can only wonder at what cost. Reports of the alien bases on the far side of the Moon say some look ancient and are in ruins. Photographs seem to show this as well. It would appear extraterrestrials on the Moon did not escape all this unscathed by any means.

10. In the aftermath, reconstruction attempts were made by survivors, both human and alien, it seems. The survivors, forced to be hunter-gatherers and primitive farmers simply weren't capable of much more than mere survival. They were too busy working just to get by to accomplish much.

The mighty engines of the Nephilim, whatever their nature might have been, once used to move giant stones, were no more. The stone monuments of the post-flood period were smaller, less impressive, much fewer in number, and mere shadows of what had come before. Many of the old ones were now under water. The Age of Stone Monuments was over, as if, as several archaeologists have said, people had just abandoned building them simultaneously all over the world.

Humans began to make a comeback during this stagnant period, even as the Nephilim, what few remained, continued to disappear. Humans, as their numbers swelled, began to take control. Judging by the written texts of the Old Testament, the cuneiform writings of the Sumerians, the Babylonians, etc., the extraterrestrials, deprived of their technology and otherworldly contacts were mere castaways, but little more.

Even so, being long-lived, it was a slow process of decline. Few in numbers to begin with, though, without their technology to back them up, they could no longer be a voice in human affairs to any real extent. The antediluvian period was over. Humans now occupied places on the *List of Kings*, where once had reigned gods or demigods.

However, some very few would seem to have survived even as recently as about 4000 years ago, as with Goliath, of David and Goliath, along with some others scattered around the planet, including in the New World. Now they are gone. That is, unless the rumors of the Yeti, and Bigfoot are true. These might be the last vestiges of a now all but vanished species.

What followed? Well, we have much the same situation as with the fall of the Roman Empire. At first, many were happy the Romans were gone from their lands. Yet, many still clung to Roman style and customs. For example, in the fifth century CE, it was a fashion for the nobility of Britain to still wear their hair cropped short and to be clean-shaven. This was in the fashion of the Romans who had since departed. Roman civil laws and customs were still very much a part of various civilizations around Europe, as well, despite the absence of the Romans themselves.

Still, the inevitable had to happen. Without Roman armies, Roman engineering, and the reinforcement of Romans themselves being present, the situation rapidly deteriorated. Romans no longer built roads; roads that tied communities together. Without a central authority, warlords, along with minor kings and their minor kingdoms, came into being. They filled the power vacuum that once had been filled by Rome. This was known, perhaps erroneously, as the Dark Ages. Some strides were made in certain respects, but when it came to law, order, safety of the citizens, wide communication and trade, all of Europe had been plunged into a very backward state.

There's ample evidence to think the same happened after the fall of the first civilization before the Great Flood, as evidence supplied in this book shows. After 10,000 BCE. and for over 6000 years, people struggled. These people scrabbled for existence among the giant ruins of those that had come before them.

As with Europe, and especially Britain after the Fall of Rome, those who had survived the collapse of the Nephilim civilization quickly forgot almost everything about that prior culture in their need just to get by every day. The people of the interregnum after the Great Flood had over 6000 years to forget and they did.

Eventually, as history seems to attest to, humanity reached sufficient numbers where their own civilization could take off. This was when the so-called "overnight explosion" of civilization occurred in history at about 3500 BCE. It continues to explode today.

CONCLUSION

We have examined all the parts of the timeline in detail. In summary, moving back from the present to 12,000 years ago, we have mentioned many things. It is important to remember that other researchers, including other archaeologists and geologists, as well, are now contesting much evidence claimed by mainstream archaeologists for this period. In some cases, as we have seen with the Great Pyramids of Giza, evidence of their true age is hard to come by and so mainstream archaeologists just sort of "assigned" them to times, based on minimal evidence, as with the pyramids being tombs.

Yet, there is nothing of a funerary nature in the way of hieroglyphics inside the Great Pyramids to show this is true, as with *all* other tombs in Egypt. A lack of any hieroglyphics in itself is very odd. In addition, there are no funerary objects to be found, except in the case of one pyramid, which has what archaeologists call a sarcophagus, but even this is highly questionable.

Archaeologists are human. Being human, they often do what they accuse UFO/ancient alien researchers of doing. That is, they will go to some lengths try to make things the way they want them to be, to make things fit their theories.

For example, because they decided pyramids are tombs, the names they have given chambers within the pyramids refer to similar things found in real tombs. Therefore, chambers in pyramids have names like the King's Chamber, or the Queen's

Chamber. They have done this without any evidence that these chambers were used for such a purpose at all! However, by referring to everything within the pyramid as if they were things in a tomb, archaeologists try to *make it seem* as if the pyramid is, in fact, a tomb, when it does not really seem likely they were. Wishing something was so, and saying it is so, still does not make it so. Moreover, using such a naming method is misleading, at best, for it implies something is true that very well may not be, or for which there is absolutely no evidence to suppose it is so.

The blunt fact is we have almost no evidence to prove the pyramids were meant as tombs for pharaohs. We have no writings, no pictures, nothing that tells us that this was their purpose. We also have a good deal of evidence to suppose they might be older than archaeologists say they are. This comes from a variety of sciences. These include, but are not limited to, meteorology, paleontology, geology, and yes, even archaeology.

An example of this? The Sphinx. The Sphinx clearly has water erosion marks on it. In other words, water formed them. It's as simple as that. Yet the Sphinx is in an extreme desert region. Therefore, this could only have happened in two ways. The first is tiny bits of water over a vast amount of time could have caused the erosion of the Sphinx. However, because of the dry, desert-like nature of the Giza Plateau for thousands upon thousands of years, this would make the Sphinx very old, indeed.

The second way is for the Sphinx to have been built in a time when there was more rain. This is the more logical choice of the two, because frankly it is less hard to explain the age of the Sphinx that way. Even so, we're still talking in the area of the space of time having to be 10,000 years and probably more. A number of bona fide researchers have come to this conclusion.

So although we must understand that mainstream archaeology has done the brunt of the work in discovering our history, we also have to understand that they don't always come to the correct conclusions.

Archaeologists don't have answers for many strange things. Göbekli Tepe and other such ancient structures are examples of this lack of answers. Do remember, with regard to Göbekli Tepe that ancient monument, one associated with the story of the Garden of Eden itself, was not only constructed thousands upon thousands of years ago, but for some reason was later deliberately buried. One can only assume it was in order to protect the site. The question is from what and why? Archaeologists have no clue.

There is another question as well. How did primitive peoples struggling to survive under extremely adverse conditions in the most nascent of times manage to build these things? Where did they find the time, the energy, resources, and the necessary numbers of people to construct such difficult projects? Think of the massive size of the platform at Baalbek and the platform at the Temple of the Mount in Jerusalem. We can't even build those things now, that without it being a tremendous effort involving thousands of people at times upon tons of special equipment. Yet, we are expected to believe tiny settlements of humans somehow managed these incredible feats?

Remember, Archaeologists are the one who set the parameters of the timeline. Yet, we have contradictions, major ones. Either these ancient people were much more advanced than archaeologists say, or they simply did not have the capability of building these things. Either way, something has to give.

There are other questions archaeologist either sidestep completely, or dismiss out of hand. For instance, did giants exist? Again, based on the available evidence, they, or something very much like them, must have existed, or how do we account for the evidence we have found, skeletal remains, written records, oral traditions, etc? Logic also says that such beings could much more easily have constructed such giant stone monuments. In any case, either all the stories, different recorded texts, etc., are wrong, or giants did exist.

As for the Great Flood, even archaeologists will admit some type of regional flooding happened in Eurasia, as with the sudden filling and rising of the Black Sea. Moreover, yes, this might account for the legends and stories of a Great Flood in that particular region. However, it would hardly account for stories of a deluge coming from around the world to us. Archaeologists admit these are a fact, too. Again, every culture has its own version of the story. How then do we account for all the evidence that shows such a flood did take place? Do we just ignore it?

We have the evidence of sunken cities and civilizations. Whether we are speaking of almost mythical places, such as Plato's Atlantis, the drowned City of Ys, or verified sites, such as Dwarka, the Pyramid of Yoniguni, or others, we have physical proof of many such sunken sites, and so what must have been a worldwide culture.

Evidence includes the styles of pyramid construction, the fact they are found worldwide, the strange markings or writings done on objects from all over the world that are of a similar nature and style, similar legends of giants from around the world, some skeletal remains, and all the oopart findings. This is not even including the written records, as well as similar oral traditions from around the globe.

Remember, not just one culture or civilization refers to a "time before the Moon." Rather, it is many. Therefore, the evidence for all this, if not incontrovertible, certainly is very telling.

Evidence shows a worldwide civilization, as well as a Great Flood. In addition, the other events with it, the arrival of the Moon, an apparent war, seem to have brought that culture to a final ending. The fact a 6500 year Dark Ages followed for humanity also seems to add strong credence to this theory. After all, it would take a long time for people to recover from such a major and devastating collapse of civilization.

With regard to our Invader Moon, we have all those writings from various civilizations referring to a "time before there was a Moon." Not only the Greeks, but also the Romans, Mayans, and many others speak of people who lived in such a time. We have the modern evidence of photographs and testimony of ancient bases on the Moon. This includes the testimony of some astronauts, satellite photographs, and the verification of various former employees of NASA, as well as various branches of government, even including officials and former officials of foreign government to tell us there were and could very well still be, aliens on the Moon.

We also have the Spaceship Moon Theory developed by two mainstream Soviet scientists, a theory, *which alone*, answers all the problems that all of the other Moon-origin theories cannot. Furthermore, the Moon's arrival and moving into orbit would have caused great tides. These would have sent waves of water onto coastlines, and perhaps so being the primary agent of the Great Flood. Weather during such ocean turmoil would have been unstable, violent, with heavy rains at times. Coastal glaciers and ice shelves would have been broken up and so swiftly melted. All this, because of the Moon's arrival in our skies. Undoubtedly, there would have been some earthquakes and geological activity as a result, as well, at least until the Moon settled into a stable orbit.

Some people argue this idea, saying the Earth has had to have tides for a long time, because of the way shorelines are, and animal life, etc. First, those people seem to forget there is more than one type of tide. We have the sun-caused tides, as well. Then there is centrifugal force of the spinning Earth, which also causes tides, which the Moon exacerbates by its gravitational pull. Strictly speaking, the definition of "tides" means just this, the distortion of an object due to gravitational pulling on it, but for our purposes, we are talking about whatever causes a rise and fall of the seas and the Earth's rotation has a hand in this.

Therefore, there was a battle beyond the stars and here on Earth, and it was an ongoing battle, it seems, one played out by some strange set of rules. One possible explanation for such a long and drawn out war is simple: relativity—if our alien interlopers didn't have faster-than light travel, or perhaps even if they did, there was still the problem of Einstein's Theory of Relativity. Time for any object as it approaches the speed of light slows down.

How does this apply to our ancient aliens? Well, any trips they made, even as sorties against the enemy, would be subject to this time differential. A ship might take off to engage the enemy, and it would be a very long time coming back, centuries or even more, perhaps. If the alien ships were able to go very close to the speed of light, this would be so. For those on board, just days or weeks might have passed. For those left behind on Earth, it could well be hundreds of years.

The result would be very much like The American Revolutionary War in some ways, with the English taking months to outfit and ship soldiers to the American colonies by sailing vessels across the Atlantic, thus giving the Americans time to recover from the last battles, and so prepare for new enemy arrivals. Wars at the time were slow affairs because of the problem of traveling slowly. The same may have held true for the Pre-Adamite Civilization.

This would explain a number of other things about the Pre-Adamites, as well. For one thing, why they used stone in their building programs so much. A civilization that built with stone, would build a very lasting infrastructure, one that could endure the great amounts of time between visits to our world and still keep functioning, and be there when their ships returned. This could well be the reason for the incredible "overkill" in building the platform at Baalbek in Lebanon, and the platform for the Temple of the Mount in Jerusalem. The aliens had to have assurances the structures would still be there for them on return trips, even if countless years, decades, or centuries had passed between visits, Earth time. In other words, the aliens had to build to last. Their "spaceports" still had to be there for them upon their return.

This relativity of time could also be one of the things accounting for tales of the longevity of some of these "children of the gods." If some of these extraterrestrials left Earth and then came back on a regular basis, centuries could have passed on Earth each time, while only days, weeks, or months might have gone by for them. For those left on Earth, humans, it would seem as if Methuselah, Noah, Enoch, and others lived very long lives, indeed.

An alternative to this might have been they had a natural longevity, being a hybrid species. Or, they might have had their lives artificially enhanced and so lengthened with medical science. Although this could also be true, or at least partially true, the time dilation theory, where relativity plays a big part, seems the most reasonable. This one thing answers a number of questions, including the extreme longevity of the Pre-Adamite civilization, which might well have spanned not just thousands of years, but perhaps millions.

Furthermore, it would explain the relatively small population of the Pre-Adamites. These beings came to Earth in ships. If they came and went on a regular basis, they simply wouldn't have had a chance to do a great deal of inbreeding with us. In fact, by the time of their next arrival on Earth, their outpost/colony world, they might already have become the stuff of legends and myths to the natural natives there, meaning us. They could well have been absentee landlords, so to speak, who only left a skeleton crew behind them each time they left. Earth, it seems, may well have not been that important to them, being nothing more than a glorified mining outpost.

However, it seems the Pre-Adamites had an uneasy rule. Evidence points to enemy races constantly having skirmishes with them, if the various myths and legends are at all true. Moreover, the vedic texts, as well, speak of just this sort of situation. They also speak of the human population being restive and rebellious.

If so, what a strange world it must have been—those with the ability to traverse interstellar distances, able to use advanced technology, and so wield great power over a larger native or indigenous population. It puts one in mind of the British when they controlled India, had it as their "jewel in the crown" of their colonies. The British were vastly outnumbered by the native Indian population, yet they remained in control for a long time. This could well be how the ancient aliens controlled Earth. A worldwide government with a slave or labor population to do their bidding.

Then is all ended. The ultimate war broke out between the alien species. Again, this war was fought in space and on the ground. At some point in the proceedings, our Moon arrived, a powerful weapon of destruction if it had alien bases on it. The Moon would literally control the high ground. Additionally, it seems it did just that.

Whoever was in control of the Earth fought back. However, it seems the odds weren't in their favor any more. The arrival of the Moon seems to have been a decisive factor. The mere arrival of it triggered massive problems on Earth for the Pre-Adamites.

The Invader Moon and those on it eventually won. The Nephilim, or whatever we wish to call them, giants, aliens, demigods, our long-time masters and leaders, were no match for what amounted to a death star hovering in their skies. Being a real life event, I suppose there were attempts at counter attacks, rallies, and endeavors to win various battles, and some might have been won, but Pre-Adamites lost in the end. The Great Flood finished what the rain of fire started. Citizens of Earth had to take shelter wherever they could find it from the bombardment.

Now, we seem to be a race with amnesia. We seem to have forgotten our real past. Like those first survivors who stumbled around amidst the mighty ruins of what had gone before, we do very much the same thing now.

We stand in awe at the massive number of stone monuments, and the sheer size of them, and wonder how they came to be. We fiercely debate the origins of such mighty monuments. All the time, we have completely forgotten of another time, "before the Moon," extraterrestrials and the Nephilim, who once strode our world.

Now people look up at the moon in the sky and admire it as a goddess of the night. We have completely forgotten our invader moon, that celestial object which brought such terror to the Earth and wreaked such havoc upon it at one time.

We should remember something else, as well. Throughout all the stories, whether biblical, Sumerian, Greek tales of their gods, etc, there is one thing that shows through repeatedly. The gods, or at least most of them, did not want humans to have knowledge. Those gods, angels, demons, or whoever, who did give us this knowledge, were terribly punished.

Remember, there were two trees in the Garden of Eden. There was the Tree of Life, and the Tree of Knowledge. The Tree of Knowledge was forbidden to us.

In conclusion, consider this question: What did these gods of old, these angels or aliens, have against us humans acquiring knowledge? The answer, of course, is they feared us having such capabilities. They didn't want us to have them for some reason, some very important reason, if the penalties for giving us such information were so extreme.

Now, at last, we are acquiring knowledge at a phenomenal rate. The sum total of human knowledge doubles every few months, or less. The genie of knowledge is out of the bottle. What will all this wealth of information ultimately mean for our world, our future, and us?

Only time will tell, but it seems that after millennia of trying to halt humans from acquiring such knowledge by those from "out there," they have at last failed, or perhaps saw the futility of trying to achieve their goals. However, what we should never forget, and never dare to forget, is that extraterrestrials may very well still occupy the high ground. They could still control possession of our Invader Moon. This means, what they did once to Earth, they could well do again. What they might do, or can do to us, may make all the difference.

Are extraterrestrials a serious threat? Did they do all this book says they did? Well, the evidence supplied seems strongly to suggest they did. However and as always, in the final analysis, the readers must decide for themselves.

There is final question we should also consider. Is the acquiring of knowledge worth it? Or might the penalties still be too high? One day, perhaps in the not too distant future, we may well have this answer.

ABOUT THE AUTHOR

Bestselling and award-nominated author Rob Shelsky is a longtime UFO investigator, as well as a Field Investigator for MUFON. His science fiction trilogy, The Apocrypha, has been nominated for The Manly Wade-Wellman Award.

Rob has written many books on the topics of UFOs, ancient aliens, the Hollow Moon Theory and much more. When finished for the day, he likes to sit in the garden, sip a glass of Merlot, watch the sunset, and contemplate his next book.

SELECTED REFERENCES

Charles, R.H., *The Book of Enoch* (Society for the Promotion of Christian Knowledge)

Davidson, G.A., *Dictionary of Angels* (The Free Press)

Childress, D. Hatcher, "Ancient Indian Aircraft Technology" in *The Anti-Gravity Handbook* (Adventures Unlimited Press, 2003)

Howard, Michael and Nigel Jackson, *The Pillars of Tubal Cain* (UK: Capall Bann, 2000)

"10 Mysteries That Hint At Forgotten Advanced Civilizations" *Listverse* http://listverse.com/2013/04/12/10-mysteries-that-hint-at-forgotten-advanced-civilizations/

"Adam's Calendar: Oldest Megalithic Site in the World?" *Ancient Origins* http://www.ancient-origins.net/ancient-places-africa/adam-s-calendar-oldest-megalithic-site-world-003160#ixzz3jr62sUBf

"Amazing Discovery, a 200,000 Year Old Metropolis in Africa" *Viewzone.com* http://www.viewzone.com/adamscalendar.html

"Ancient Humans Bred with Completely Unknown Species" Ancient Origins http://www.ancient-origins.net/news-evolution-human-origins/ancient-humans-bred-completely-unknown-species-001059

"Ant People of the Hopi, The" *Ancient Origins* http://www.ancient-origins.net/myths-legends-americas-opinion-guest-authors/ant-people-hopi-00927

"Artifacts from the Pre-Flood World—Fallen Angels Proof" *Truthaddsup Always YouTube Channel* https://www.youtube.com/watch?v=yFz1tnKot9w

"Black Knight Satellite" *Wikipedia* https://en.wikipedia.org/wiki/Black_Knight_satellite

"China Releases Moon Footage of Alien Bases" *UFO mania—The Truth is Out There* http://ufothetruthisoutthere.blogspot.pt/2014/03/extraterrestrials-china-releases-moon.html

"Circular Ruins and Satellite Archaeology on Ancient Aliens" *Jimmy Fisher YouTube Channel* (Excerpt from *History Channel's Ancient Aliens* Season 5x08 "The Mystery of Nazca.") https://www.youtube.com/watch?v=fRYxYnHZUzA

"Circular Ruins and Satellite Archaeology on Ancient Aliens" *Jimmy Fisher YouTube Channel* (Excerpt from *History Channel's Ancient Aliens* Season 5x08 "The Mystery of Nazca.") https://www.youtube.com/watch?v=fRYxYnHZUzA

"Circular Ruins in Peru" *Google results page* https://www.google.com/search?q=circular+ruins+in+Peru&tbm=isch&tbo=u&source=univ&sa=X&ved=0CDYQsARqFQoTCKnJs7uY_MYCFQSsHgodY2OP9w&biw=1024&bih=641

"Controversial Claim by Geologist: Mysterious Tracks in Turkey Caused by Unknown Civilization Millions of Years Ago" *Ancient Origins* http://www.ancient-origins.net/news-mysterious-phenomena/controversial-claim-geologist-mysterious-tracks-turkey-caused-unknown-020489#ixzz3o8RCoc8q

"Engraved Stone Dating Back 30,000 Years Found in China" *Sci-News.com* http://www.sci-news.com/archaeology/article00755.html

"Fossil Suggests Egyptian Pyramids and Sphinx Once Submerged Under Sea Water" *Epoch Times* http://www.theepochtimes.com/n3/1274558-fossil-suggests-egyptian-pyramids-and-sphinx-once-submerged-under-sea-water/

"Genographic Project/Why Am I Neanderthal?" *National Geographic* https://genographic.nationalgeographic.com/neanderthal/

"Giant Human Skeleton unearthed in Varna, Bulgaria" *Ancient Origins* http://www.ancient-origins.net/news-history-archaeology/giant-human-skeleton-unearthed-varna-bulgaria-002787#ixzz3jjtjkvlA

"Governments are HIDING Aliens, Claims Former Defence Minister: Paul Hellyer Urges World Leaders to Reveal 'Secret Files'" *Daily Mail* http://www.dailymail.co.uk/sciencetech/article-3051151/Governments-HIDING-aliens-claims-former-defence-minister-Paul-Hellyer-urges-world-leaders-reveal-secret-files.html#ixzz3o8VOeXf1

"Hoax or not? Underground Tunnel Discovered Between Sicily and Calabria" *Italy Magazine* http://www.italymagazine.com/news/hoax-or-not-underground-tunnel-discovered-between-sicily-and-calabria#sthash.iet1bvom.dpuf

"Initial DNA Analysis of Paracas Elongated Skull Released—With Incredible Results" *Ancient Origins* http://www.ancient-origins.net/news-evolution-human-origins/initial-dna-analysis-paracas-elongated-skull-released-incredible#ixzz3jjzLOGlI

"Meeting mummy in the valley of the giants" *China Daily* http://www.chinadaily.com.cn/2014-05/14/content_17505601.htm

"Mysterious Structure Found at Bottom of Ancient Lake" *CNN* http://www.cnn.com/2013/04/19/world/meast/israel-ancient-structure-mystery/

"Mysterious Tunnels" *Rense.com* http://rense.com/general62/msytun.htm

"NASA Employees: Huge Alien Structures and UFOs on Dark Far Side of Moon" *Inquisitr* http://www.inquisitr.com/2158158/nasa-employees-huge-alien-structures-and-ufos-on-dark-far-side-of-moon-video/#YfOj44J52maKvPHm.99

"New Genetic Study Suggests the Pharaohs of Ancient Egypt Were Alien Hybrids" *Locklip* http://locklip.com/the-pharaohs-of-ancient-egypt-were-alien-hybrids-new-genetic-study-suggests/

"Oopards, Smithsonian, We Have a Problem" *thearrowsoftruth.com* http://thearrowsoftruth.com/ooparts-smithsonian-we-have-a-problem/ (As of 10-09-2015 this url is not available).

"Prehistoric China" *Ancient Wisdom* http://www.ancient-wisdom.com/china.htm

"Scientist Unravels Mystery of Coral Sea's Ghostly Sandy Island" *The Washington Post* http://www.washingtonpost.com/ national/health-science/scientist-unravels-mystery-of-coral-seas-ghostly-sandy-island/2013/04/14/76316606-a508-11e2-8302-3c7e0ea97057_story.html

"Secret Ancient Subterranean Tunnels And Caverns Across America: Who or What Were Our Ancestors Hiding From?" *MessagetoEagle.com* http://www.messagetoeagle.com/ secret-ancient-subterranean-tunnels-and-caverns-across-america-who-or-what-were-our-ancestors-hiding-from-2/#ixzz3o873TFMW

"September 2013 AOM: Decoding the Hidden Ruins of Southern Africa—Discovering the True Cradle of Humankind" *Graham Hancock* http://www.grahamhancock.com/forum/ TellingerM1.php

"The Sumerian King List Still Puzzles Historians After More Than a Century of Research, The" *Ancient Origins* http://www. ancient-origins.net/myths-legends-asia/sumerian-king-list-still-puzzles-historians-after-more-century-research